HOW CAN I GROW AS A

FOLLOWER OF

JESUS?

Biblical, Actionable Practices
for Discipleship

TIM WIEBE

For my parents, Kerwin and Jan Wiebe.

Thank you for modeling a lifetime of pursuing and growing in Christlikeness.

OTHER BOOKS BY THE AUTHOR

What Does It Mean to Follow Jesus?: A Clear, Biblical Picture of Discipleship

PRAISE FOR *HOW CAN I GROW?*

Tim Wiebe's second book in his discipleship series has the same practical, substantial, biblical feel. The spiritual disciplines presented are accessible for everyone. This book should be a helpful boost to the believer who wants to continue the journey of grace-filled, Christ-honoring discipleship.
Dr. Greg Carlson, professor emeritus of Christian Ministries and Leadership, Trinity International University

Dr. Wiebe's work on spiritual disciplines is a fresh perspective on essential habits of the vibrant Christian life. In a clear and accessible style, he neither over promises nor undervalues the intentionalities of "working out our salvation." Christians of any level of maturity will benefit from Dr. Wiebe's observations and insights—which I know to be not only his theory but his own personal practice as well.
Dr. Colby Kinser, District Superintendent, Midwest District EFCA

If ever one hoped to cultivate the kind of growth that is both meaningful and strategic, Tim's words certainly serve to that end. With well-researched biblical insight, you will be encouraged to thoughtfully engage and eventually craft a personal strategy around each game-changing discipline that steadily shapes the heart, renews the mind, and overflows into a life marked by depth, meaning and mission. Whether you're in the early stages of exploring the way of Jesus or have been a Christian for a long time—this book will equip you to grow on purpose.
Emily Taylor, author of *Firmly Planted*

I often meet people who are either brand-new to the faith or just beginning to take their walk with Christ more seriously. From now on, this is the book I'll put in their hands. If you want a resource that blends solid theology with clear, practical guidance, look no further—this is it.

Chris Winegar, Lead Pastor, LifePoint Church

I couldn't wait to get my hands on this follow-up to Tim's first book, *What Does It Mean to Follow Jesus?* Accessible and deeply anchored in Scripture, *How Can I Grow as a Follower of Jesus?* is a trustworthy companion for discipleship. I will be using this both personally and as a resource for discipleship with others!

Christina Dart, Director of Women's Ministry, Brookside Church

Rooted in Scripture and pastoral ministry, Tim Wiebe's *How Can I Grow* is a practical and accessible guide to spiritual formation for anyone who wants to grow. This is a great starting point for training in godliness.

Dr. Matthew LaPine, Director of Equipping, Citylight Church, Omaha, NE; author of *The Logic of the Body*

Tim's second book on discipleship invites Christ-followers ready for growth to cultivate the Christlike mindset and lifestyle with joy, devotion, and purpose.

Jonathan C. Musonda, Lead Pastor, Fairview Baptist Fellowship, Lusaka, Zambia

CONTENTS

INTRODUCTION

I'm guessing you picked up this book titled *How Can I Grow as a Follower of Jesus?* because in some way this is a question you're asking. Maybe you're an interested seeker who is exploring the person of Jesus Christ and Christianity, and you're wanting to know more about spiritual practices that the Bible talks about and Christians have been observing for millennia. Maybe you've been following Jesus faithfully for decades, and you know that anchoring yourself more deeply in fundamental spiritual disciplines is valuable (after all, we never graduate from the basics). Maybe you've just recently placed your faith in Jesus, and you want clarity on how you can grow in this most-important relationship.

Wherever you're at with this question, "How Can I Grow as a Follower of Jesus?," I've been praying that this material serves you well. If spiritual growth is something you're interested in and believe is valuable, I'm writing this book for you.

More specifically, I'm writing this book for people who want to grow spiritually but aren't sure where to start or how to get traction. I'm writing for people who would benefit from

1

revisiting certain fundamentals about how to grow as disciples (or followers) of Jesus Christ—either to stir your own heart or as you come alongside others.

I'm writing this book with the church family I serve in mind. I can think of names and faces of people I've interacted with over the twenty-plus years I've been in ministry—people who proclaimed faith in Jesus and who *wanted* to grow spiritually and experience the full life Jesus offers (John 10:10). As I've listened to and interacted with others as a pastor, most often their questions about spiritual growth or obstacles to growth aren't about a lack of desire. The people I have in mind have *wanted* to grow, or at least they've known it's important (they've "wanted to want it").

But as important as desire is, other factors are also essential for growing in Christlikeness. In other words, even when someone has the *desire* for growth, that doesn't mean growth is automatic and easy. (I'll say this from the opening pages and you'll see it repeatedly through the book because of how important it is: Spiritual growth is never automatic or easy. *We don't drift into spiritual maturity.* Constant attention to this goal and intentionality are needed.) Certain hang-ups need to be addressed to cultivate a life of meaningful growth as followers of Jesus. If these hang-ups aren't addressed, they can stunt, slow down, or stall out the process of Christian growth.

For some, their hang-up is *direction.* For those who lack clear direction about Christian growth, they need a biblical **picture** of following Jesus that instills confidence that they're moving in the right direction and valuing the right things as they pursue spiritual growth as Christians.

Others hit the hang-up of personal *discipline.* They want to grow and become like Christ, but they simply need to know how to do that. They would benefit from biblically informed **practices** that serve the goal they desire—growing as disciples and seeing Jesus make a noticeable difference in their lives. They need vision for how these practices, or tools, serve the larger goal of Christlikeness, rather than becoming mechanical ends in themselves, hoops to jump through, or boxes to check off.

Or their hang-up may be *drive*. There is a simple desire to grow, but those who hit this hang-up need to be reminded that the fuel that propels growth is not white-knuckled effort or "just trying harder" to earn God's acceptance. If this mindset is what is driving spiritual growth, it will lead to either discouragement (if you fail) or arrogance (if you externally succeed at maintaining the spiritual disciplines). Rather, the fuel that propels true growth is the good news of the gospel—God's amazing grace demonstrated to undeserving sinners who place their faith in Jesus Christ. We practice the disciplines and pursue spiritual growth not to *earn* God's acceptance but *out of* God's acceptance of us, through faith in Jesus' finished work. This humility-filled, gratitude-laden "gospel drive" has no bottom to its reservoir and is robust enough to keep us going through life's difficult terrain.

The people I have in mind over decades of ministry have wanted to grow. They have desire. What they need is clarity about *direction*, practical tools to help with *discipline*, and the essential, never-to-be-forgotten truths about the gospel that *drive* this pursuit. These factors are often the bread and butter of how I try and come alongside them, as we all work to advance Jesus' commands to be disciples and to make disciples (see Matt. 4:19; 28:19).

I'm confident you picked up this book because you have some interest in growing as a follower of Jesus yourself. I believe this interest you have is God-given, and I encourage you to lean into it, wherever you're starting from. You may be on the very front end of following Jesus. You have placed your faith in Him and now are wanting to grow as His follower. (If you've not yet taken this step of placing your faith in Jesus, I'd encourage you to visit www.twowaystolive.com, a website that spells out very clearly why this decision is so important and how you can do so. Consider including a Christian friend in conversation about this.)

Or perhaps you've been following Jesus for most of your life; you can't really remember a time you didn't know Jesus. You're wanting to stoke a desire to grow personally. Or you're looking for tools that can serve you as you disciple others.

My goal now is to take what I've shared with others in face-to-face meetings or classroom environments—lessons and truths I've benefited from myself, and need to keep reminding myself of—and share them with you.

The lessons that I share fall broadly within these categories I've already introduced—*direction, discipline,* and *drive.*

My first book, *What Does It Mean to Follow Jesus? A Clear, Biblical Picture of Discipleship,* focused primarily on direction—providing six "Cs" that clarify a picture of what it means to grow in Christlikeness. These six Cs of conformity to Christ are commitment, communion with God, community with others, character, conduct, and commission. (Appendix 1 in the book you're holding summarizes each of these six Cs.)

This book focuses on the area of "discipline"—getting practical on how we can grow as disciples and make disciples. The goal of this book is to provide concrete practices—rooted in God's Word and motivated by God's grace—that cultivate spiritual growth through selected spiritual disciplines. In what's ahead, chapter 2 through chapter 6 will look at the disciplines of Bible engagement, prayer, fasting, solitude, and commitment to the church. Each chapter will look at the selected discipline through the lens of a particular passage of Scripture, as I want to root these disciplines deeply in the truths of God's Word.

Then, these chapters will also include a section called "Tools for the Toolbox." This section will get practical, providing tips and ideas for how to get traction with these disciplines in your life.

Importantly, chapters 7 and 8 include "disciplines" that are perhaps less *practice* and more *perspective*—the perspective of confidence that motivates perseverance (chapter 7) and the perspective of a missional mindset (chapter 8). These perspectives can at times be overlooked in a simple listing of spiritual disciplines, but they must not be neglected. A confident dependence on God and a heart for multiplying disciples should be "baked into the batter" of our pursuit of growth as a whole.

The conclusion of this book then ties things together, providing a sort of "workshop opportunity" for you to revisit what you've learned and very directly reflect on how these disciplines and perspectives connect to spiritual formation in key areas of life.

As you read either of these books (or both!), I hope you see a healthy, consistent, and frequent dose of gospel "drive"—as the good news of Jesus' work propels our pursuit both of *who* we're becoming (direction) and *how* we get there (discipline).

Please know that I need the truths of this book even as I share them with you. My earnest desire is to serve you and your good desire to grow in Christlikeness, and that this book contributes to that greater end.

HOW CAN I GROW AS A FOLLOWER OF JESUS?

CHAPTER 1
SPIRITUAL DISCIPLINES: *WHAT?* AND *WHY?*

I'm a huge fan of Husker football, the college team of the University of Nebraska at Lincoln. I was a high schooler in the 1990s when the Huskers were at a high point in their program's development. They won three national championships in four years (1994, 1995, 1997). The head coach of Nebraska football in the 1990s, Tom Osborne, remains ranked among the best coaches in college football history. In 2019, ESPN ranked Osborne fourth in the 150 greatest coaches in college football's 150 year history.[1]

What made Nebraska football the powerhouse that it was? Any answer to that question would need to list a number of contributing factors: Osborne's brilliant offensive mind, the players they recruited, and more. But in his book *The Legacy of Leadership*, Tom Osborne peels back the curtain and reveals another difference-making piece of their success—and it's something we can all learn from.

Osborne points to the strength and conditioning program, which began at Nebraska in 1969. Here's what he says:

> This transformed football at the University of Nebraska from three months of football in the fall and a month of spring football into a year-round training regimen involving weight-lifting, flexibility, and agility workouts combined with good nutrition.
>
> Over all those years, I saw that people who were most disciplined in their approach to conditioning were the most successful. If you weren't in the weight room and if you didn't practice hard, you had no chance.[2]

Did you catch that? The factor that led to success was their approach to conditioning and practice. Coach Osborne knows what every other coach and athlete and musician and performer knows: You play how you practice. If you want to play well, you need to practice well.

Here's what all this talk about conditioning and practice has to do with the *what* and *why* of spiritual disciplines. In 1 Timothy, the apostle Paul is all about helping his closest protege "play well" as Timothy leads the church in a city called Ephesus. First Timothy was written toward the end of Paul's life—he knows he's passing important ministry lessons and truths along to one of his key successors. This letter is dripping with personal flourish, essential topics, and intensity.

And in the middle of this playbook on building a healthy church and serving faithfully, check out what Paul says in 1 Timothy 4:7–8: "Train yourself to be godly. For physical training is of some value, but godliness has value for all things, holding promise for both the present life and the life to come."

Wait: Did Paul really just say "train yourself to be *godly*"? When we slow down on that word *godly* and think about it, it likely registers some reaction in each of us. You might hear the word "godly" and conjure up an image of a super-Christian (however you define that) and then think, *I can't be that.* If this describes your reaction to godliness, you may feel discouraged by the goal Paul puts in front of us. Or you might conjure up an image of someone who lives a boring life that drains the joy out of rooms and always has a disapproving frown on their face. If this is your reaction to being godly, you think, *I don't want to be that.* You're disinterested in this goal Paul sets.

Whatever your knee-jerk reaction to the idea of godliness, I encourage you to keep reading. Don't put the book down yet. As we dig into this passage, we'll see how good of an idea it is to train yourself for godliness. You *can* see progress and it *is* worth it.

In the rest of this chapter, we'll press more deeply into 1 Timothy 4:7–8 by asking a few valuable questions about these verses. We'll ask, "What is true godliness?" and we'll see that true godliness isn't boring. Rather, true godliness is both inviting and compelling. We'll ask, "Why does godliness matter?" Paul gives us clear motivation—showing us that training for godliness is the best, most lasting investment you can make. And then we'll introduce the question the rest of this book will address, "How can I grow in godliness?" We'll lay some important groundwork about the spiritual disciplines that will carry us forward into the chapters ahead. Motivated by God's grace and energized by His Spirit, you can "train yourself to be godly".

Here's the difference studying this passage and answering these questions can make: You can move *from* "I don't want to grow in godliness" or "I don't see the value in it" *to* "I want that, and I see that it's the best way to live." Wherever you are in the life of following Jesus, if you listen well to 1 Timothy 4:7–8, by the end of this chapter you'll have your motivation stirred or refreshed for growing in godliness.

What Is True Godliness?

So first question, "What is true godliness?" What are we training for when Paul tells us to "train yourself to be godly"?

Does it mean you have to stay inside and pray all day or that the only acceptable pastime is Bible reading, a life where you remove yourself from the world around you? No.

Think of some of the godly people we read about in the Bible: Abraham and Joseph and Moses and Ruth and King David and Esther and Peter and Paul. Nothing about their lives was boring. They had jobs, families, responsibilities, leadership positions, problems, and goals. They're the heroes of the Bible! They're the people we want to be like. And they were godly.

Does training ourselves for godliness mean that we have to do something to earn our way to God? Also no.

"Training for godliness" doesn't establish a program we need to complete in order to earn a relationship with God. We know that because the apostle Paul who wrote 1 Timothy 4:7–8 to "train yourself for godliness" is the same apostle Paul who wrote Ephesians 2:8–9: "For it is by grace you have been saved, through faith—and this is not from yourselves, it is the gift of God—not by works, so that no one can boast."

The good news here is that we don't have to clean ourselves up before God accepts us. God accepts us because we trust in what Jesus has *done*, not because of what we *do*. The only way any of us can have a right relationship with God is because of Jesus, by God's grace.

So those are some things "training for godliness" doesn't mean. But what *does* it mean? That word for "godliness" in 1 Timothy 4:7–8 literally means "the honoring of God in everyday life."[3] It means we have a big view of God that directs and impacts how we actually live our daily lives in identifiable ways—whether you're a student, a skilled tradesperson, an executive, a parent, or wherever else you may be coming from.

Here's another way to think about it: "Godliness" here is basically synonymous with how followers of Jesus talk about "Christlikeness." After all, if you want to see Someone who was perfectly godly (that is, perfectly honoring God in everyday life), look at Jesus! Christlikeness is both following Christ's example in our own lives (see John 13:14–15, 34; 1 Cor. 11:1; Eph. 4:32–5:2; Phil. 2:5; 1 Peter 2:21–23) and allowing the new life Christ makes available to be increasingly formed in us, from the inside out (see Rom. 6:3–4; Gal. 4:19; Eph. 4:20–24). Throughout this book I'll be using "godliness" and "Christlikeness" interchangeably.

In an earlier book, *What Does It Mean to Follow Jesus?*,[4] I've teased out areas of life that should be impacted as we follow Jesus. To help paint a picture of what godliness/Christlikeness looks like, here are the six areas of life that together help us understand what it looks like to grow in godliness/Christlikeness (see also appendix 1, where these 6Cs are included with a bit more explanation):

- **Commitment:** Following Jesus changes my allegiance.

- **Communion with God:** Following Jesus opens up intimacy with God through knowing Christ, in the most satisfying and enriching of relationships.

- **Community with others:** Following Jesus means belonging and transformed relationships.

- **Character:** Following Jesus will change me from the inside out.

- **Conduct:** Following Jesus transforms the way I live and what I actually do.

- **Commission:** Following Jesus gives me purpose and sends me out on mission.

We mustn't forget *godliness* as the goal of our discipline, and here's why: If we forget this goal in our "training," then it will either become an end in itself or it will be directed toward other ends. Both of these alternate possibilities are dangerous. If training becomes an end in itself, our spiritual disciplines and the effort we spend will become meaningless. We'll be going through motions but won't be getting anywhere—think of a car spinning its wheels in the mud.

Or if our training is directed toward other another goal (i.e., something other than godliness), we'll soon realize that it can't satisfy. Instead, it can twist our hearts. Wrong goals may be self-righteousness (feeling good about myself and looking down on others because of what I'm doing or not doing, see Luke 18:9–14) or people-pleasing (working hard for the approval of others but not God). We must keep in mind Paul's full command here: Train yourself for *godliness*.

Here's the bottom line: The picture of godliness that the Bible provides isn't boring or unattractive. I talk with people frequently who want to grow in these qualities: experiencing intimacy with God, belonging with others, transformed character, and making an eternal difference in the world. When we see that godliness is exemplified in these qualities that we already know we want and need, suddenly true godliness isn't something to be avoided. True godliness becomes something to pursue and to grow in. True godliness is something to desire.

Why Does Godliness Matter?

Let's drill a little more deeply into that idea of *pursuing* and *desiring* godliness by looking at our next question: "Why does godliness matter?" What difference does it make? Answering this question will add additional fuel to our pursuit of and desire for godliness. Paul provides crystal clear motivation in 1 Timothy 4:8: "For physical training is of some value but godliness has value for all things, holding promise for both the present life and the life the come." In other words, physical training is good and important; training for godliness has an even better good.

Just think of it: Godliness holds promise for the present life. I often wonder if Christians need to make it more clear that we believe that following Jesus is the best way to live. If you feel empty or unsatisfied or restless, Jesus can fill that void like nothing else can. As the fourth-century church leader Augustine said so famously, "Lord. . . . You have made us for Yourself, and our hearts are restless till they find their rest in You."[5]

That doesn't mean a life of godliness is easy. You won't get everything you want. Following Jesus isn't always going to feel like a nice downhill coast on a sunny day. (In other words: biblical Christianity is not the prosperity gospel.)

No, following Jesus is not easy. Yet at the same time Christians proclaim that following Jesus is the best way to live now. How can this be the case?

Following Jesus *anchors our identity*. On the one hand, our identity in Christ keeps us in our place as His disciples and willing servants, so we don't fool ourselves into thinking we're the kings or queens of the universe. In our world that can so often elevate and isolate self in anxiety-inducing ways, our identity in Christ reminds us we belong to Him and only understand ourselves rightly in relationship with Him. Yet in the very same breath, Christian identity affirms that we are graciously forgiven and fully accepted by God the Father through faith in Jesus (see Rom. 4:7–8; 5:1). God loves us and nothing can separate us from that love (Rom. 8:37–39; Eph. 3:14–19). We are friends of Jesus (John 15:14–15).

Following Jesus offers *purpose*. Jesus gives us a mission that is bigger and better than anything I'd choose for myself. You can help advance the purposes of God in your sphere of influence in ways that others can't. Your life has meaning.

Following Jesus instills a secure *hope*. This hope includes an assurance that God will complete His good purposes in us, whether we can always see it or not (see Phil. 1:6). This hope includes the promise of a glorious inheritance that will never perish, spoil, or fade (1 Peter 1:3–4). The future God has prepared for His people is a place free of grief and pain; a better-than-you-can-imagine place of wholeness and perfection in God's restored creation and life-giving presence (see Rev. 21:1–5). While this hope surely is fulfilled in eternity (more on this in a minute, when we look at Paul's statement that godliness holds promise for the life to come), this hope should set our direction and motivate our perseverance today.

Imagine how living in line with Christian identity, purpose, and hope impacts situations you're facing right now. Christian identity, purpose, and hope make a difference. Or back to the words of the apostle Paul: Godliness holds promise for this life, right now—in the way you live today, and this week. Do you believe this? How can this truth shape your life?

What a compelling life Jesus invites us into! We're not done yet, though. There's more we need to see about the promise of godliness.

Godliness also holds promise for the life to come. One of my favorite movies is *Gladiator*. Russell Crowe plays the part of

Maximus, a Roman general stripped of his authority who becomes a gladiator fighting for life and freedom in the grotesque Colosseum games. One of the great quotes of the movie comes early on, when Maximus says to an army of troops right before battle, "What we do in life echoes in eternity." Of course it energizes the troops and off they go roaring into battle.

When Paul says godliness holds promise for the life to come, it's almost like he's saying something similar, but with an important twist: "*Who you are* in life echoes in eternity." Whatever else Paul means by v. 8, Paul is clearly telling us that we're not just training for training's sake. I believe this training is one way for us to be faithful stewards of our time and efforts as we await our Lord's return and the rewards He then shares (see Matt. 25:14–30). As you train yourself for godliness, this disciplined pursuit is worth it in the most important, lasting, eternal ways possible. Growing in godliness holds promise for this life and the life to come.

All right, so we've seen what true godliness looks like and why growing in godliness is worth it. Now how do you actually do it?

How Can I Grow in Godliness?

The answer is simple but it is not easy. You train yourself for it. That verb "train" in 1 Timothy 4:7—"train yourself to be godly"—is from the Greek word *gumnazo*. You can hear the word "gymnasium" in it. Just think of the regimented training and the consistent drills that happen at the gym or fitness club. The word is one of effort, sweat, and pushing yourself past your comfort zone to get one more rep in.

In other words, Paul is saying you're not going to drift into godliness. It doesn't just happen. Just like you need to train intensely for a marathon if you're going to compete successfully, so too you need to train intensely to grow in godliness. This is training that never stops, and it's not something anyone else can do for you. Train yourself for godliness.

In the following chapters of this book, we'll get specific on what this training involves by focusing on individual spiritual disciplines that can cultivate growth in godliness. The biblically rooted, time-tested disciplines that we focus on here are the following: Bible engagement, prayer, fasting, solitude, local church involvement, perseverance, and disciple-making.

Before we get into these individually, a few comments by way of orientation will be helpful.

First, my goal in this book isn't innovation but faithfulness. There are many good books on the spiritual disciplines.[6] I want to simply add my voice to the chorus that champions discipleship for the experience of Christians, the edification of the church, and the equipping of believers with tools they can use in discipling others.

Second, you may have also heard other terms used to describe this training for godliness (e.g., holy habits, spiritual practices, spiritual exercises). I don't have any issue with these other terms but have chosen to retain the more traditional "spiritual disciplines" language because of how closely it aligns with Paul's *training* language in 1 Timothy 4.

Third, I need you to bring yourself into this book. In other words, this book is intended to lay a foundation on which you build. Here's some of what this may mean:

- If you're brand new to this idea of training for godliness, think of one small step of application you can take into each of these disciplines as you go. If you need help with what practical application may look like, ask someone who's been following Jesus for a while.

- If you've been following Jesus and are familiar with these disciplines, has your training gotten imbalanced in any way—such that you're strong in some of these disciplines but weaker in others? Or is there someone you can meet with—to equip them to grow in these disciplines?

- A great way to "bring yourself" into this book is by reading it with others—whether a church small group of 6–8, an interactive classroom environment in your church, at home with your spouse and teenage kids, or in a reading group of 2–3 others from your work or neighborhood. Sharing insights, discussing takeaways, and working through your questions with others will help you internalize and "own" what you're learning in lasting ways. Your questions and comments will benefit others in the group too! To help facilitate this sort of interaction, I've included some questions at the end of each chapter that can guide your group.

One final comment by way of orientation. Don't forget what these spiritual disciplines are *for*. We don't do them to earn our salvation. They're not ends in themselves. Our goal isn't just to know a lot about the Bible or fill up a few more hours with serving. Paul tells us to "train yourself to be godly." Our goal is practical godliness—that over the course of time (even if it's perhaps more slowly than we want), we'd grow in looking more like Jesus.

Conclusion

It's important for us to understand that God's posture in all of this isn't one of angry demand and frustration. Nor is it one of disappointment because of all the ways we've fallen short in these disciplines or messed up prior to this. God doesn't give up on you because you trip up or fall short in these areas.

God's expression is one of love, and He's cheering you on as you train yourself for godliness—even if you stumble and even if you feel like you're moving at a snail's pace. And the reason I can say that is because of the good news of the gospel. We don't do any of these things we've been talking about to earn favor with God. Everything we do is a response to the grace we've already been shown in Jesus' death for our sins on the cross—grace you've been offered and can experience by placing your trust in Jesus and choosing to follow Him (see Rom. 10:9–10; Eph. 2:8–9; Titus 3:5–6).

Let me say it as clearly as I can: Everything we do to train in godliness rests on and is motivated by what Jesus has already done.

Questions for Reflection and Discussion

1. What made you pick up this book and start reading? What are you hoping to get out of it?

2. Name a performance you've been a part of (an athletic event, a musical performance, etc.). How essential was practice for a good performance? Why?

3. Think more about the performance you shared in the previous question. How did knowing what you're practicing or training *for* help keep you motivated to train?

4. According to 1 Timothy 4:7, what should Christians be training for? As a group, discuss what "godliness" looks like in practical terms. (Need some help? Check out Matthew 22:36–40 and Galatians 5:22–23. See also appendix 1 on "6C Discipleship.")

5. Look at 1 Timothy 4:8. What motivation does Paul give for training in godliness?

6. Do you have any examples from your life of how training in godliness "holds promise for this present life"?

7. How does training in godliness hold promise for the life to come?

8. The word for "train" in 1 Timothy 4:7 is an athletic word, carrying the ideas of effort, strain, and pushing yourself past what's comfortable. In other words, we don't drift into godliness; we must be intentional about training ourselves for it. Why is this important to keep in mind?

9. Scan the Table of Contents. Which of the spiritual disciplines listed there are you more familiar with? Will any of these disciplines be brand-new for you to study?

10. "Train yourself for godliness" requires lots of <u>doing</u>. In the midst of this, why is it essential to ground our right standing with God not on what we *do* but on what Jesus has *done* (see Ephesians 2:8–9)?

11. What practical step will you take to apply one thing you've learned in this chapter?

CHAPTER 2
BIBLE ENGAGEMENT: DELIGHT AND DILIGENCE

I grew up with a lot of exposure to God's Word, the Bible. Some of my earliest memories are walking into the kitchen in the morning and seeing my parents reading their Bible over a bowl of cereal to start their day. I remember my parents leading my two older brothers and me spiritually—opening up the Bible or devotional books with us after supper or before bed and talking about what we learned for a few minutes. We attended church on Sunday mornings and Wednesday nights, where God's Word was faithfully taught.

I'm so grateful for this exposure now, but I didn't always appreciate it in the moment. I was the kid that couldn't wait till family devotions were done so I could get on to something else. I made my way through sermons by looking at the pictures in my kid's Bible and the maps at the end. There was nothing uniquely special about the Bible to me back then—or at least I wasn't living like there was. My actions and my attitude showed that I pretty much thought the Bible was just another book. I could hold it at arm's length, and I'd be fine.

Then during my sophomore year of high school, a lot of things converged in my life in a short period of time and the gospel became vivid—a living, personal relationship with Jesus took root in my life in some fresh ways.

My youth pastor in high school, John, saw what was going on in my life and invested a lot of his time in me. I remember one experience like it was yesterday. John took me out to lunch one day and then we ended up back at the church building. He brought me into the worship center, filled with blue pews that I'm sure were awesome and cutting-edge in the 1990s.

John sat me down with a Bible, a pen, and a piece of paper with some questions on it and lots of blank space. He said something along the lines of "If you want to really follow Jesus, you need to know your Bible and get it in your life; you can't grow as a Christian apart from this book." And then he told me to read Habakkuk chapter 1 (I still have no idea why he chose Habakkuk, a small book in the Old Testament, as the place to point me!). While I read, he asked me to write down all the observations I saw from Habakkuk 1 and the questions I had, and that he'd be back in thirty minutes.

Over the next thirty minutes as I studied Habakkuk, my approach to God's Word went from black-and-white to ultra-HD, or from 8-bit pixelated graphics (who else remembers pixelated Mario?) to the modern photorealism we see in gaming graphics today.

A whole other world opened up to me, and I was hooked on the value of God's Word. The thing that had changed was how I approached this book! I discovered there's truth in here that I need. That the Bible can stand up to my best questions. That it leads me toward full life the way God designed it.

Since then, I want to keep passing along what I was told and that I've now experienced again and again over the course of decades: If you want to follow Jesus and experience full life the way He's designed, you need to be in the Bible. You can't grow as a follower of Jesus apart from this divinely given, divinely inspired, and divinely authoritative book. You need to get into the Bible in such a way that the Bible and its truth get into you.

Enter: Psalm 119

Looking back, I see now that I discovered the truth that Psalm 119 is all about: **God's Word is a great treasure for our lives today.**

I know that statement is pretty simple and straightforward, but if you asked me about the bottom line of this entire chapter, that's the truth I want to drive home. Here's why this is so important: If we can get this—that God's Word is a great treasure and that it's for us still today—that's the pivot point that opens up so much growth as followers of Jesus.

Psalm 119 is made up of 176 verses—it's the longest chapter in the Bible, and longer than many whole books of the Bible. In all but a handful of these 176 verses the psalmist says something about God's Word, connecting it to his current life and what he's facing. And one of the dominant threads that runs throughout everything the chapter says is that God's Word is supremely valuable. God's Word is a great treasure.

How can we talk about the value of God's Word when so many people think this book is offensive, outdated, intolerant, and full of contradictions? These are important issues. And there are Christian scholars who have addressed these questions well.[7]

Or perhaps the Bible still remains an artifact to you. An object to be studied at arm's length. But not much more than that.

The Bible itself won't let us settle for this view of Scripture as abstract, antiquated, or irrelevant. We need to be fair and let the Bible speak for itself. The Bible makes (and can back up) claims that it is a book like no other, inspired by God Himself as His revelation of who He is, what He's doing, and what that means for you and me. The Bible is God's Word for us, unique in authority and useful for growing in godliness and good works.

Two passages from the New Testament introduce us clearly to the God-inspired origins of this book, its authoritative nature, and its timeless relevance:

> All Scripture is God-breathed and is useful for teaching, rebuking, correcting and training in righteousness, so that the servant of God may be thoroughly equipped for every good work. (2 Tim. 3:16–17)

> For the word of God is alive and active. Sharper than any double-edged sword, it penetrates even to dividing soul and spirit, joints and marrow; it judges the thoughts and attitudes of the heart. (Heb. 4:12)

The message of these verses is unmistakable. Scripture is from God. It's useful—equipping us for good works. It works in us personally and actively, and there's no expiration date on that. The Bible isn't some antiquated, lifeless book.

Psalm 119 adds its own strong voice to this chorus, pointing us toward the value and worth of God's Word that has everything to do with our lives still today.

Since we don't have space to cover all 176 verses in Psalm 119 (though I encourage you to read the whole psalm in one sitting!), I've chosen one verse to help us discover the worth of God's Word in a way that's consistent with the whole psalm.

We'll be focusing on Psalm 119:16: "I delight in your decrees. I will not neglect your word."

We can divide the verse into two parts very neatly: We've got the first half that talks about delight and the second half that talks about the diligence God's Word deserves. Both delight and diligence underline the value of God's Word. When something is valuable we delight in it. And when something is valuable we give it our close attention. Let's dig in a little more and spend time on each of these halves.

God's Word Is a Source of Delight

First, we see right there in the first half of Psalm 119:16 that God's Word is a source of delight. Read that sentence again slowly, out loud: God's Word is a source of delight.

For some people, that statement doesn't compute. When you think of what God's Word does, maybe you think of studying and lots of deep thinking. Or maybe when you think of God's Word you think of rules, regulations, and boring conversations.

But delight? Probably not.

However, delight *is* what comes to the psalmist's mind when he thinks of Scripture! Just in this one psalm, the NIV translation connects the word "delight" to God's Word nine times.[8] (And there are many more times the idea of delight is conveyed apart from the word being used![9]).

The question we need to ask, then, is "Why did the psalmist find delight in God's Word?" We can find an answer to that question right here in Psalm 119. Straight from this psalm, we see at least four benefits of God's Word that led to the psalmist's delight in it.[10]

One benefit is that **God's Word offers freedom**. So often we can think that God's Word is restricting and that sin (doing what we want) is freeing. We think following God's Word will make our lives smaller. But look with me at Psalm 119:133: "Direct my footsteps according to your word; let no sin rule over me." Sin doesn't free us; it exercises its own sort of harsh and demanding rule over us. If we're honest with ourselves we know this diminishing, handcuffing reality of sin. Certainly any addict would tell you this: What first promised freedom quickly brought chains. To the psalmist, it's God's Word that's freeing. "I will walk about in freedom, for I have sought out your precepts" (Ps. 119:45). God's Word offers freedom.

Another benefit of God's Word is that **God's Word offers stability**. Here are three verses in Psalm 119 that drive this point home:

> If your law had not been my delight, I would have perished in my affliction. (Ps. 119:92)

> You are my refuge and my shield; I have put my hope in your word. (Ps. 119:114)

> Great peace have those who love your law, and nothing can make them stumble. (Ps. 119:165)

Reflect on some of the words in those verses: God's Word sustains us in our trials. God is our *refuge* and our *shield*. God's Word brings hope and offers peace. All of these statements underline the stability that God's Word brings. God's Word keeps us anchored to God and His promises when the waves of our lives hit hurricane level.

I've seen this sustaining strength of the Bible. As a pastor, I talk with a lot of people in counseling settings, and over the years I've spent a fair amount of time in hospital rooms. In so many of these situations, I'm trying to minister to people who have just had the bottom drop out of their lives—severe suffering and trial. I've seen the stabilizing influence God's Word can bring as it reminds people of who God is and what He is doing. I've seen the peace God's Word brings as people learn of the hope we have because of Jesus, and the promises of God.

What's the stabilizing force in your life? Is it a relationship that you're hoping can carry the weight of everything? Are you depending on circumstances or the achievement of some goal to hold all the weight of how you're really doing? What happens when the relationship lets you down in a big way or a small way? Does your whole life start to crumble? What happens if you miss the goal—you don't get into the college you want, or you're passed by for the promotion? What happens when circumstances are difficult?

Don't forget the truth of Psalm 119:65 that we just read: "Great peace have those who love your law, and nothing can make them stumble." We want that peace! We want that resilience! Let's not miss how the psalmist experiences it: This peace and resilience follow those that love God's Word.

Next, **God's Word offers direction.** Again, this benefit stands out in Psalm 119:

> Teach me knowledge and good judgment, for I trust
> your commands. (Ps. 119:92)

27

We all want knowledge and good judgment—to know we're making good decisions and living with wisdom instead of foolishness. Where does the psalmist find this wisdom? By looking to God in His Word.

> Your word is a lamp for my feet, a light on my path.
> (Ps. 119:105)

Verse 105 paints such a vivid picture. Think of the difference a headlamp makes when you're walking through an unfamiliar place. A little bit of light on the path forward makes such a difference!

> The unfolding of your word gives light; it gives understanding to the simple. (Ps. 119:130)

What an inviting, hope-filled verse! The Bible isn't just for the learned; the Bible is accessible to the simple. We don't need to be wise or book smart before we can benefit from the Bible; the Bible is what makes us wise.

Again and again, Psalm 119 reinforces the direction that God's Word gives.

A fourth benefit we find in Psalm 119 is that **God's Word leads us to God Himself.** Here's what I mean by this point: God's Word is the primary way that God has revealed Himself to us. This book isn't an end in itself. But at the same time, we need to come to terms with the fact that if we're seeking God and if we want to know Him, we can't ignore His Word. If we wanted to know God apart from His Word, that would be like us trying to get to know someone but ignoring everything they tell you about who they are! God's Word leads us to God Himself. This is what came to life for me that afternoon I was in Habakkuk as a sixteen-year-old. It's through the Bible that we meet and better know the living God of the Bible.

> I seek you with all my heart; do not let me stray from your commands. (Ps. 119:10)

How does the psalmist seek God Himself with all his heart? Through His commands.

> You are righteous, LORD, and your laws are right. (Ps. 119:137)

God's character and God's Word are consistent with each other.

True freedom. Stability. Direction. A greater knowledge of and relationship with God Himself. These benefits motivate us to read God's Word. When we hear somebody delight in something and talk it up—whether it's a good movie, a new restaurant, or a person—that usually piques our interest. The way the psalmist talks about God's Word makes me want these things God's Word offers. Whenever our motivation lags in reading God's Word, let's remind ourselves of everything God's Word brings to the table: freedom, stability, direction, and greater knowledge of God Himself.

Let's return to Psalm 119:16: "I delight in your decrees." This is what we have been talking about—delighting in God's Word. Now let's focus on the rest of the second half of the verse: "I will not neglect your word." What we see here is that God's Word captures our attention. God's Word deserves our diligence.

God's Word Deserves Our Diligence

According to the Oxford English Dictionary, the word diligence means "constant and earnest effort to accomplish what is undertaken" or "persistent application and endeavor."[11] Synonyms for diligence include alertness, carefulness, and earnestness.[12]

So what does it mean to approach the Bible diligently, with "constant and earnest effort"? I'll focus here on one thing this approach involves: We make time to read Scripture closely.

When my children were much younger, my wife and I would read to them before bedtime. Since my wife knows some Spanish, one of our books was a Spanish book titled *Los Chicharos Amigables*. It was your basic small children's book: a board book with just a few words on each page and lots of pictures.

Now, this book that was entirely in Spanish is a book they would sometimes want *me* to read to them. I could look at the words. I could kind of pronounce them. I would read them the book out loud when they asked me to.

And I wouldn't understand any of it. My eyes saw the words, but I couldn't tell you what any of it meant.

Sometimes I wonder if this is how we approach the Bible. We look at the pages. We can say the words. But if you ask us what we read, we wouldn't be able to really answer.

Our excuse, however, can't be that we don't know the language. We have great translations in Spanish and English and so many other languages. For some of us, our issue is that we don't read the Bible closely.

So what does it mean to read the Bible closely? To read the Bible closely, we need to start with three words: *observe, interpret,* and *apply*.[13]

1. Observe: What does the passage you're reading say? We read slowly enough to see what's actually there. Dallas Willard challenges us on this: "It is astonishing how little of the Bible is known . . . by people who profess to honor it. If we do not know it, how can it help us?"[14] If we're going to be formed by the Bible, we need to know what the Bible actually says. Not what we think it says or even what we want it to say. We need to know what the Bible actually says. Making progress in this effort requires both spending time in the Bible and observing what's actually there.

2. Interpret: What does the passage mean? How would we restate the biblical author in our own words—in a way that the biblical authors themselves would agree with? Interpreting the Bible well requires that we pay attention to context. This starts with the immediate literary context in which the passage we're studying is situated—the verses before and after it, and the message of the biblical book. Over time, we learn more about literary genres of the Bible, and the cultural and historical contexts of the Bible—helping us better understand the meaning in a way the biblical authors intended. This step of interpretation is where our own careful thought, a study Bible or a trusted commentary,[15] and good Christian teachers or other spiritually mature believers can be helpful.

3. Apply: How does this message take shape in my life? How does it influence the way I think? What I believe about God? How I treat others? The actions I take? This step of application is so important! Second Timothy 3:16–17 says the Bible is useful and equips us for good works—we apply its truth in a way that makes a difference in how we actually live Monday–Saturday, and in the ways we interact with others in the world around us. This application can take many shapes, including transformed actions, renewed thinking, or adjusted relationships.

Bible Engagement: Tools for the Toolbox

Let's spend some time getting practical. What can it look like to approach God's Word with delight and diligence? Here are some ideas to get you started—or keep you moving in a healthy direction.

First, as you open God's Word or before you begin listening to it, **focus on relationship**. The Bible is written by God to help us know Jesus and live in a way that honors Him. The Bible isn't some artifact to study at arm's length. It's not just about collecting information for trivia night. It's not a rulebook designed to take away your fun. God gave us the Bible to reveal Himself, so that we might know Him and live the full life He designed for us. As you engage the Bible, remember that it's written to form and strengthen a vibrant relationship with the living God (see John 5:39–40).

When I'm firing on all cylinders with my own Bible engagement, this focus on relationship takes explicit shape in a prayer before I begin reading. I'll pray something as simple as "Lord, as I spend time in your Word today, may I know you better as the Author when I'm done." Or in Psalm 119:18, the psalmist gives us another prayer that can focus our hearts every time we open God's Word: "Open my eyes that I may see wonderful things in your law." This prayer is dependent on God Himself (relationship!) for insight into His Word and points us toward the realization that the most "wonderful things" in God's law for us to see are truths about God Himself (relationship!).

Make a commitment to engage the Bible out of desire to grow in meaningful relationship with the Lord who reveals Himself in His Word.

Second, press into all the ways you can **immerse yourself in God's Word.** The Navigators—a Christian ministry that helps people grow as disciples—has helpfully created something they call the "Word-Hand Illustration,"[16] which highlights five methods of learning from the Bible. These five methods are included below, with a few sentences after each of my own explanation.

- *Hear*: There are numerous good ways to stay exposed to biblical truth through simply hearing it. We can listen to audio versions of the Bible. You hear God's Word proclaimed and explained through faithful teachers.

- *Read*: This method highlights the straightforward (and important) task of reading the Bible. And for this "read" method, I often encourage reading the Bible in large chunks—at least a full chapter at a time. Even better, read multiple chapters at a time. Devote 20–30 minutes to simply reading Scripture and you'll be amazed to discover that you can finish whole books in one sitting or make significant progress through a book. Reading Scripture this way can give you a powerful sense of the flow of a book and literary connections within the book.

- *Study*: This method is where you slow down and focus on a smaller passage. You read it repeatedly. You follow the "observe, interpret, and apply" steps outlined above. A great way to facilitate study is to bring a pen and paper to the task. Write down observations and questions. Push yourself to summarize the passage in your own words, in a way the biblical author would agree with. Write down one to three ways truth from the passage should take shape in your life. Over the course of time, these written (or typed) study notes can accumulate into a powerful resource for you and others. (See also Ezra 7:10; 2 Tim. 2:15.)

- *Memorize*: This is exactly what it sounds like. Most commonly we memorize verses or small passages that anchor us in truth about who God is or how He wants us to live. If you want a "stretch goal" I encourage you to memorize whole chapters of the Bible. (Looking for a place to start? Try any of these: Pss. 1; 16; Rom. 8; Col. 3.) In Philippians 4:8 Paul urges us to think on things that are true, noble, right, pure, lovely, admirable, excellent, and praiseworthy. God's Word is all of these things, and the work it takes to memorize Scripture will press us to focus on it and experience its renewing effects (see Rom. 12:2).

- *Meditate*: The best picture I have for biblical meditation is marinating meat like chicken or steak. When meat soaks in a marinade and that's done well, the marinade will permeate the meat so that you can't taste the meat without getting a hint of the marinade. That's what meditating on the Bible means: God's Word has so permeated our hearts—we've soaked in it so deeply—that every part of us has the taste of God and His Word (see also Josh. 1:8 Pss. 1:1–3; 119:97). This step of *meditation* is really the culminating effect of all the other methods: We've been so immersed in God's Word that it works itself into us and out from us seamlessly. What nineteenth-century preacher Charles Spurgeon said of seventeenth-century author John Bunyan can be true of us. Spurgeon said Bunyan's blood was "bibline, the very essence of the Bible flows from him."[17] That is, when you pricked Bunyan, he "bled God's

Word." He was so full of biblical truth it just flowed out of him. May that be true of us as well.

As we immerse ourselves in the Bible, let's benefit from what each of these methods offers, rather than narrowly limiting ourselves to only one of these methods.

A third step of practical application for engaging God's Word faithfully is this: **You're not done until you respond.** This is the Bible engagement tip that holds our feet to the fire with what passages like Matthew 7:24–27 and James 1:22–25 talk about—not just hearing but also applying God's Word. Our lives are different because of what we read. Our marriages look different because of what we read in the Bible. Our friendships look different. The way we approach our jobs or our studies is different. We let the truth of God's Word influence our thoughts and attitudes, our relationships, and our actions. Our goal isn't just to "get into the Bible." Our goal is to "get into the Bible in such a way the Bible gets into us."

Conclusion

Let's look at Psalm 119:16 together one more time: "I delight in your decrees. I will not neglect your word." What I love about Psalm 119 is that it shows that God's Word is a treasure that directs the way the psalmist lives his life. He approaches Scripture like he wants it and needs it.

Are you tired of being owned by sin and wondering if there's a better way to live? Are you wondering if you can find stability and peace in uncertain circumstances? In what areas of life do you need direction? Do you wonder if you can know God better than you do right now?

God's Word provides all of these things. What a source of delight! And God's Word deserves our diligence: approaching it well, immersing ourselves in it responsibly, and responding faithfully.

I want to leave you with a picture that encourages me in this direction again and again. Because as much as my view toward God's Word changed as a sixteen-year-old, my approach can still ebb and flow. I need to fuel my hunger for this book, so my appetite stays fresh.

I'm so grateful that I have been able to visit Zambia about a dozen times and meet pastors who approach their Bibles like the psalmist approaches his. I go there to teach them content from God's Word, but every year I walk away being challenged by them and how they approach the Bible.

Here's how hungry they are for the Bible: A lot of them travel more than 100 kilometers (some much farther than that) to come to the pastors' training we offer—and they don't often come by car. They hitch a ride when they are able but probably spend a significant part of the distance walking or riding a bike.

Then, for 8–9 hours a day for a week they sit on picnic benches or hard seats in a small room while we teach them. (Not an ideal learning environment.) They would often sleep on mats on a hard floor in a single room with lots of other guys.

Put an American in that situation and we'd be complaining after thirty minutes about the conditions. (We probably wouldn't even sign up in the first place!) But these pastors eat it up. They do this joyfully, four times a year for three years, because they want the Bible to be central to their lives and their ministries.

I'll say it again: I go to teach them some content from the Bible, but they have challenged me far more with their approach to the Bible. They model what I want to keep growing in. What I encourage you to keep growing in: "I delight in your decrees. I will not neglect your word" (Ps. 119:16).

Questions for Reflection and Discussion

1. Describe any exposure you had to God's Word (the Bible) growing up. Briefly summarize your attitude toward the Bible when you were younger.

2. An overarching message of Psalm 119 is that "God's Word is a great treasure for our lives today." Reflect honestly on your personal reaction to this message of Psalm 119. Do you agree? Why or why not?

3. How does the culture around us respond to the worth of God's Word? Provide concrete examples if you can.

4. Psalm 119:16 talks about "delighting" in God's Word. Is this idea of "delighting" in the Bible new to you? Why is approaching God's Word with this posture important?

5. Scan Psalm 119 and try to come up with at least 6–8 reasons God's Word should produce delight. Which of these reasons stands out to you most? Why?

6. Psalm 119:16 highlights how God's Word deserves our diligence. Compare a casual approach to God's Word with a "diligent" approach. What practically might it look like for you to give God's Word your "diligence"? What steps can you take in this direction beginning this week?

7. Read John 5:39. Jesus teaches that God's Word is not an end in itself but should point to Him. Why is this focus important to keep in mind?

8. Imagine you had to explain to someone how the Scriptures point to Jesus. What are some of the points you might include in your explanation?

9. "God's Word is a great treasure for our lives today." What needs to happen in your attitude and your daily routine for you to live into the truth of this statement?

10. What other questions or comments do you have about anything covered in this chapter that you'd like to discuss?

11. What is your biggest takeaway from what you've discussed so far? Is there a practical step you can take to apply what you've learned?

CHAPTER 3
PRAYER: PRIORITY AND PRIVILEGE

This chapter on prayer is the one I struggled the most to write. It was the last chapter I completed as I chipped away at this book, going back and forth with what to say. My issue wasn't primarily with the shape or structure of the chapter. My issue wasn't with substance—there's a wealth of biblical teaching on prayer.

My struggle is practice.

When I encounter what the Bible teaches on prayer, I realize how much I'm just scratching the surface of what's available. When I read books on prayer or quotes from notable Christians across the centuries, I want to experience what they describe so beautifully and powerfully.

When I look back on my practice of prayer just over the last few weeks, I see gaps in my prayer life—both in terms of what I pray for and how often I pray. I can be a task-oriented person, and if I'm not "checking off a box" or doing something with immediate, noticeably tangible results (in other words: I'm not praying), I'll feel guilty that I'm not doing what I'm supposed to be doing. (Yes, I know how hollow that sounds.) I can too easily drift into self-sufficiency, where I mistakenly think success rests on my shoulders and I effectively forget the triune God. I'm pretty good at offering to be the helper, but I stink at being the one to ask for help. I've not modeled a life of dynamic, dependent prayer for my family. This is humbling for me to admit. I struggle to practice a life of prayer in a consistent and compelling way.

I'm convicted by the words of J. I. Packer in his *Knowing God*: "We must learn to measure ourselves, not by our knowledge about God, not by our gifts and responsibilities in the church, *but by how we pray and what goes on in our hearts*. Many of us, I suspect, have no idea how impoverished we are at this level. Let us ask the Lord to show us."[18]

More than perhaps any other chapter in this book, I'm writing this chapter as a fellow-traveler toward a life more devoted to prayer. I'm writing this chapter for myself—to soak in beautiful truths of the Bible regarding prayer, in a way that stimulates my own practice of prayer.

The Priority of Prayer Throughout the Bible

To get right to the point, prayer is communicating with God. It's an essential ingredient in our relationship with Him— a relationship that's personal, interactive, and deeply dependent. To be clear, the dependence here is one-sided. We are deeply dependent on God. God is not dependent on His creation. God delights to be depended on, and He proves perfectly good, trustworthy, and faithful. Any relationship that is personal, interactive, and dependent naturally requires communication.

We'll flesh out what motivates prayer and how we can grow in devotion to prayer throughout this chapter, but first I simply want to highlight the priority that Scripture places on talking with God in meaningful relationship with Him. We see this from the beginning of the Bible all the way through to the end.

In the very opening pages of the Bible, we discover that God is a communicating God—He speaks everything that is into existence (e.g., Gen. 1:3, 6, 9, etc.). But very quickly we realize that the God of the Bible doesn't only speak to *create*; He also speaks to *relate*. God interacts personally with Adam and Eve in the garden (Gen. 3:8–9), and He interacts personally with Cain in Genesis 4:6. While each of these passages deserves close study as individual passages, the point I'm trying to make here is broader: From the earliest pages of the Bible, it is abundantly clear that there's communication between God and people.

Now let's jump all the way to the end of our Bibles. In Revelation 21, the apostle John points toward the amazing future God has for His people in the new heaven and new earth. In this restored creation where sin is no more (Rev. 21:27; 22:3), we read the following:

> And I heard a loud voice from the throne saying, "Look! God's dwelling place is now among the people, and he will dwell with them. They will be his people, and God himself will be with them and be their God. 'He will wipe every tear from their eyes. There will be no more death' or mourning or crying or pain, for the old order of things has passed away." He who was seated on the throne said, "I am making everything new!" Then he said, "Write this down, for these words are trustworthy and true." (Rev. 21:3–5)

Just look at all that relational language! God dwells "among the people." God wipes tears from eyes. He declares the renewal of everything. All of this language drives home what we've already said about a relationship with God that is personal, interactive, and dependent on Him. As followers of Jesus anticipate our eternal future, it's clear there's communication between God and His people as an aspect of this relationship.

Between these bookends of the biblical storyline, communication between God and people remains prominent. We see communication between God and Abraham (e.g., Gen. 12:1–3; 15:1–6; 18:16–25). We see communication between God and Moses (e.g., Ex. 3:1–4:17; 32:7–14; 33:7–23). The list could go on: Job, Joshua, Jonah, Hannah, David, Daniel, prophets, psalmists, Mary, Anna, Peter, Paul. Again and again and all throughout Scripture, it's clear that there's communication between God and His people. Prayer is a priority.

"But these are all the *big names* of the Bible," you might be thinking. You're wondering if God works with "average people" like us the same way. You're wondering if you can experience the presence of God in personal relationship with Him through prayer. You're wondering if you can see the power of God at work in answer to your prayers. You're wondering if prayer matters for you.

The answer is yes. Prayer isn't just for the "big names" or "major characters" of the Bible. Prayer—communicating with God in personal, interactive, dependent relationship on Him— is just as much for us as it was for them. We see this in the earliest church in Acts. Acts 2 tells the true story of "about three thousand" people placing their faith in Jesus after Peter's sermon on the Day of Pentecost (see Acts 2:1–41). The overwhelming majority of this group were "average" people whose names we'll never know this side of eternity. Yet what was one of the driving priorities of these "average" believers? "They devoted themselves to . . . prayer" (Acts 2:42). Prayer remains a priority in Acts for many other "average" Christians (e.g., Acts 4:23–31; 12:5; 13:1–3).

This priority of prayer continues in the New Testament letters. Paul commands the church in Thessalonica (full of "average" believers like us) to "pray continually" (1 Thess. 5:17). He commands the Colossian church to "devote yourselves to prayer" (Col. 4:2). Paul invites prayer for himself more than once, leaning on other "average" believers who can join him in prayer (see Eph. 6:19–20; Col. 4:4). The apostle Peter highlights the importance of prayer to those to whom he writes (1 Peter 4:7). James commands prayer and talking with God in a variety of circumstances (James 5:1–16). Jude spotlights prayer in his letter (Jude 20–21).

Let me return to and reinforce the bottom line: Talking with God in a personal, interactive, and dependent relationship is a priority all throughout the Bible. This priority is also a privilege. What a joy it is to know we can approach God's throne with confidence, knowing that He hears us as His children (see Gal. 4:6–7; Heb. 4:16).

Is prayer a priority in your life? Do you understand the privilege it offers?

Help from Jesus on the "How?" and "Why?" of Prayer

A passage that's been especially helpful for me regarding prayer is Matthew 7:7–11. In this passage, Jesus shows us how and why we can turn to God confidently in prayer. He's helping us where we struggle—He's helping us pray!

If you feel inadequate about the practice of prayer, Jesus' words here will be so encouraging to you. Jesus gives us practical teaching on how to pray. If you're unsure about who the God you're praying to is, Jesus' words here will give you clarity and comfort. Jesus reminds us who God is, and why we can trust what He puts in front of us.

In Matthew 7:7–11 Jesus gives us two fundamental points on prayer. These points will be helpful to you if you're taking your first baby steps into a life of prayer. These points will remain helpful to you if you've been faithfully modeling prayer for decades. These are fundamental points we never graduate from; we simply move more deeply into them. So what does Jesus say that helps us with prayer in Matthew 7:7–11? Jesus teaches us (1) how to pray, and (2) who we pray to.

Let's get the passage in front of us, and then we'll look at these points individually.

> "Ask and it will be given to you; seek and you will find; knock and the door will be opened to you. For everyone who asks receives; the one who seeks finds; and to the one who knocks, the door will be opened. Which of you, if your son asks for bread, will give him a stone? Or if he asks for a fish, will give him a snake? If you, then, though you are evil, know how to give good gifts to your children, how much more will your Father in heaven give good gifts to those who ask him!" (Matt 7:7–11)

Now back to the question we're asking: What does Jesus teach here that helps us with prayer?

Jesus Teaches Us How to Pray

The three verbs in Matthew 7:7 ("ask," "seek," and "knock") are all *present imperative* verbs—that means they're commands that have an ongoing nature. It's like Jesus is saying: "Ask, and keep on asking. Seek, and keep on seeking. Knock, and keep on knocking."

The idea is persistence.

44

This may lead to a question on your part: So what are we to persistently ask for? What are we to diligently seek?

To answer that, let's not forget that this is the second time Jesus has talked about prayer in this Sermon on the Mount (the first time being in Matthew 6:5–15). In other words, Matthew's first readers—and those who first heard Jesus deliver His sermon—would have remembered what Jesus said earlier on prayer in Matthew 6 *from just minutes earlier*. It would have been very fresh in their memory, still at the front of their minds.

There in Matthew 6 Jesus gives us what we call the Lord's Prayer—where He teaches His followers how to pray. And then in the rest of that prayer, Jesus helps us know what to ask for:

> This, then, is how you should pray: "Our Father in heaven, hallowed be your name, your kingdom come, your will be done, on earth as it is in heaven. Give us today our daily bread. And forgive us our debts, as we also have forgiven our debtors. And lead us not into temptation, but deliver us from the evil one." (Matt. 6:9–13)

So what do we ask for? Among other things: We ask for God's name to be made holy, and for His kingdom to come. We ask for provision for our daily needs and forgiveness and protection. The Sermon on the Mount has already given us a great head start on what to pray for!

At the same time, God wants to hear what you bring to Him from your life right now and what's pressing on your mind this week.

I wonder if we overcomplicate prayer too much sometimes. We want our requests to sound polished before we bring them to God. We try to fit things into a formula that sounds right. We're worried about saying something the wrong way, and sometimes that keeps us from saying anything at all.

But when you think about it, *asking*, *seeking*, and *knocking* are such simple actions. Anyone can do these things. What this simplicity shows us is that Jesus isn't looking for some fancy formula. He's looking for any expression of simple dependence. Don't know exactly how to say it? Just ask! Don't know if you're asking for the right thing? Still knock!

I love this reminder from J. I. Packer and Carol Nystrom in their book on prayer: "Don't fret [about praying]; just pray. God fixes our prayers on the way up. If he does not answer the prayer we made, he will answer the prayer we should have made."[19]

Scripture has plenty of examples of short, quick, knee-jerk reaction prayers:

Right before the Old Testament leader Nehemiah has to convince the foreign king to let him rebuild the wall of Jerusalem, Nehemiah breathes a short prayer while he's in the middle of a real-time conversation with the king in Nehemiah 2.

In Mark 9, a desperate father who wants Jesus to heal his son says simply—but powerfully—to Jesus, "I do believe; help me overcome my unbelief!"

In Luke 18 a blind beggar knows Jesus is passing by and all he calls out is "Son of David, have mercy on me!"

Your prayers don't have to be like one of the Psalms. They don't have to be long, poetic, and worthy of people reading them thousands of years later. Your prayers can be simple. Just ask. Seek. Knock.

I've worked alongside a godly woman named Lorinda for close to twenty years. She serves our church with excellence and leadership in so many ways. She's so good at empathizing with people in need who come to us for help. Lorinda also walks prayerfully, and has clung to her faith through some deep, dark valleys earlier in her life. Simple, honest, desperate prayer sustained her through these difficult times.

Lorinda and I were in a conversation about prayer recently, and here's what she had to say about her practice of simple prayer:[20]

> Sometimes I've prayed simply, "hang on to me" or "hold me" or even, "I can't find you!"

> Sometimes I've prayed, "Lord please be louder! I'm so overwhelmed with grief, fear, worry, sadness . . . it's become so loud in my heart that it's drowning *you* out . . . that I cannot hear you or feel you! And I know you're there because I believe . . . but please help me *feel* that you're there."

> That may not feel like a traditional prayer. At the end of that—a lot of times—nothing has changed. But I know I've been talking / begging / sobbing with my friend.

When you think of praying a simple prayer—asking, seeking, knocking—what simple, honest, desperate prayer to God rises first to your mind? Those are the kind of things that God wants you to bring before Him!

However simple and straightforward and unpolished it may be, God wants us to ask. And keep asking.

Close readers of Matthew 7:7–8 know there's more to these verses than we've looked at so far. In these verses, Jesus says not only to ask and seek and knock, but He says that to everyone who asks, it'll be given. He says that everyone who seeks will find. What is Jesus getting at?

Jesus isn't advocating for any sort of prosperity gospel, name-it-and-claim-it theology here. The reason I say that is because of everything Jesus has already said earlier in the

Sermon on the Mount. If we're praying for more zeros on the end of your paycheck so we can live a convenient life, that conflicts with what Jesus has already said in Matthew 6:19–21 and Matthew 6:24 about not treasuring earthly things. Or if we're praying for the person who slighted us recently to "get theirs," that conflicts with Jesus' command for us to love our enemies in Matthew 5.

Jesus is assuming we're praying in line with His will—with what He's been teaching in the Sermon on the Mount.

But what happens if we're praying for seemingly good things and God still doesn't answer the way we've been asking? That question takes us right into our next point: Let's see what Jesus teaches next about who we pray to.

Jesus Teaches Us Who We Pray To

We see "who we pray to" most clearly in Matthew 7:9–11:

> Which of you, if your son asks for bread, will give him a stone? Or if he asks for a fish, will give him a snake? If you, then, though you are evil, know how to give good gifts to your children, how much more will your Father in heaven give good gifts to those who ask him! (Matt. 7:9–11)

Jesus is imagining an everyday situation every one of His hearers could relate to—a situation where a son asks his dad for something the son legitimately needs. Bread and fish were staple foods. Jesus says of course the father will give him what he needs. No father is going to trick his son with a stone or try to harm him with a snake.

In other words, a son can trust what his father puts in front of him.

Jesus then drives His point home: If imperfect, sinful dads do this for their sons, how much more will our perfect God—our heavenly Father as believers in Jesus Christ—give good gifts to His children?

That idea of thinking of God as a Father may be difficult for some people. Every earthly dad falls short in some way or another. But some are especially cruel and negligent. Perhaps you were abused or neglected. Or your dad was selfish. Or absent. Your heavenly Father is not like your earthly dad. He is powerful and good. He is present and attentive and near to you.

If this all brand-new to you, please search the Scriptures to discover what it means that God is your Father. I know this isn't an easy switch you can just flip "on" or "off." Discover the Bible's full presentation of who God is, and make that—and not your experience growing up—your view of God.

It is a beautiful thing that God is our heavenly Father.

Check out this quote from Paul Miller: "Oddly enough, many people struggle to learn how to pray because they are focusing on praying, not on God."[21]

When we focus on God—our heavenly Father who gives good gifts—it invites prayer. It invites trust. God as our heavenly Father who gives good gifts means we can trust what our Father puts in front of us.

I know that's a bold statement. As you read this, you may be going through tremendously difficult, trying times. I don't want to minimize that at all.

Neither do I want to back away from calling us to trust in God.

I know that showing this trust in what God gives isn't always easy. I finished seminary in 2005, and I hadn't landed my "what's next" job yet. I was married, and we had just had our oldest son days before graduation—so the stakes were high. I needed to find something.

I had turned down an offer for a great job that didn't seem like the best fit for me, and all my eggs were in the basket of a church in Kansas I was talking with. I was praying for this to work out, and everything seemed to be lining up. I wanted to provide for my family—a good desire! The church was and is a solid church—no concerns or red flags. The role was something I was interested in and thought I could contribute to meaningfully. I was progressing in their rounds of interviews and getting along with people I met.

I was asking God for this to happen. Ask, seek, knock, right? Everything about it seemed good.

And then it didn't happen. I still remember where I was when I got the call: the church was turning me down because they wanted someone with more experience.

I look back now and understand their decision. I probably would've made the same one had I been in their shoes. But in the moment, it felt like a big deal to be sent back to square one. A wife, a kid, and no job. Zero other prospects.

So I moved back to Omaha where I had grown up, and Brookside Church—the church where I had grown up—threw me a bone with a part-time internship. In one sense, I was tremendously grateful. In another sense, it was humbling to me—I seemed to be climbing "down" the ladder, not "up"!

And then after a few months, they offered me a full-time job. And now Brookside has been a gift to me and my family for twenty years.

From my vantage point now, I'm so glad God didn't give me what I was praying for when I was interviewing in Kansas. I thought I knew what I wanted, but God knew what I needed. I needed to learn to trust Him.

Tim Keller gets it right: "God will only give you what you would have asked for if you knew everything he knows."

Who do we pray to? Our heavenly Father, who gives us good gifts. We can trust what our Father puts in front of us.

In what way do you need to trust what God is putting in front of you?

Or maybe you can't yet see what God is putting in front of you. You can't yet see how the story you're in the middle of right now will take its next turn. The truth of Matthew 7:9–11 is still comforting and trust-building: How can seeing God as a good Father help you cling to Him with trust?

Prayer: Tools for the Toolbox

Jesus' teaching in Matthew 7:7–11 is so helpful. What a privilege prayer is! Now let's continue to keep our eyes on practical application. What are some "tools for the toolbox" that can help us grow in prayer and dependence on God?

In no particular order, here are six overlapping "helps" that have served me in my practice of prayer. I'm not perfect at any of these, by the way. I aspire to grow in these things. My goal isn't to add what feels like an overwhelming obligation when you think about implementing all six of these in your life. My goal is to help you envision what growing in a life of prayer can look like; if one or two of these seem especially helpful to you, focus on those.

One practical help for me is to **more directly connect my Bible reading and prayer life.** Too often, we can treat Bible reading and prayer as sealed off from each other, "dueling monologues" where God is talking to us (Bible reading) and then we're talking with God (prayer)—and often these "monologues" aren't connected in any way. But what if we approached Bible reading and prayer more like a dialogue? For example: As something stands out to us in our meditative Bible reading, we can linger to talk with God about whatever that is. We can confess ways we don't measure up. We can pray for opportunity and strength to apply what we read. We can praise God for who He is. On and on the list could go. The goal here is to see Bible reading and prayer as interwoven, allowing each to feed the other.

Another way to apply this connection between Bible reading and prayer is to let the prayers of Scripture give you words and categories for your own prayer life. I'm thinking here of praying through individual psalms slowly, or benefiting from the ways the Lord's Prayer can launch us into prayer, or how Paul's prayers in so many of his letters give us language we can pray for ourselves and others.[22] When my prayer life wanes for whatever reason, my first "go-to" is to return to select psalms (e.g., Pss. 16; 19; 24; 25; 27; 103; 145) or the Lord's Prayer (Matt. 6:9–13) and allow these passages to jumpstart my practice of prayer.

Another practical help for me is to **"activate the acronyms."** Over the years I've heard a number of acronyms that can facilitate prayer—the two that have stuck with me the most are ACTS (adoration, confession, thanksgiving, and supplication—supplication is a fancy word for requests) or PRAY (praise, repent, ask, yield). An acronym like this can help you experience a life of prayer that goes beyond "just asking God for stuff." Yes, God loves to hear our requests, but there is so much more to a life of prayer! God is worthy of our praise and gratitude. We have sin we need to confess. We express trust in a posture of holy surrender. One of these acronyms can help "balance" our prayer lives in healthy ways and help us experience the formative benefits of a holistic prayer life.

Yet another practical tool is to **pray with a pen in hand**. If you struggle with focus during times of prayer, having a pen in hand can help you with focus. This may mean actually writing out your prayers. (Just to be clear: These aren't for anyone but you and God. You're not writing these to publish them. Don't feel any pressure about polish, grammar, etc.) Journaling prayers also gives you the opportunity to go back and see what you've prayed for over the course of time and how God has responded.

A fourth practical tool is to find a way to **keep simple, manageable lists** to record things you want to be praying for. A system that I use (imperfectly!) is to think in terms of *daily* prayers (3–5 prayer items) and *weekly* prayers (6–7 items, about one per day). So, for example, my daily prayers include prayers for my wife and immediate family. My weekly prayers include my local church leadership (Mondays); global missions and evangelism needs I know of / partners we support in prayer (Tuesdays); health requests or care needs I know of (Wednesdays); or my extended family (Saturdays). (I'm intentionally not listing everything that's on each of my lists because *you need to create your own list*. Your list will look different.) As needs come up in one of these categories, I know I can commit to praying for them as part of these rhythms. And since on any given day I'm praying for a handful or so of items, I can do this manageably.

Fifth, for things that may not be on my official "list" just described, I have learned the value of **praying in the moment.** Certainly this "praying in the moment" includes the ongoing dependence I want to cultivate with God—the open lines of communication between God and myself that Paul is referring to when he commands us to "pray continually" in 1 Thessalonians 5:17. Prayer isn't a task we do for twenty minutes each day and then move on from; prayer is ongoing dependence and communication.

"Praying in the moment" also acts on the opportunity we have when requests come up to pause, in real time, and spend two to three minutes praying to God for that request *in the moment*. Ideally, if you're with the person who's asking for prayer, you can stop and ask, "Can we take a minute and pray for that now?" And then pray! If you hear about a request through text or some other means where you're not with the person, you can pause, stop whatever you're doing, and pray for the request. "Praying in the moment" can take shape in praying for specific requests alongside prayers of thanks before mealtimes, or before bedtime with kids and/or your spouse.

One more practical tool that I've found helpful is to **stand on the shoulders of others.** For me, this usually means reading (or rereading) a book related to prayer each year—to learn how other followers of Jesus approach this beautiful privilege we have in prayer. Of course, we must not substitute *reading about* prayer for the actual *practice of* prayer. For me, I've found learning from others can be a meaningful motivator to prayer (and not a substitute). I know of others that use a resource like the *Valley of Vision: A Collection of Puritan Prayers* or the *Book of Common Prayer* to provide structure and shape to their own prayer life. While resources like this can become mechanical (a danger to avoid), we must not overlook the ways they can be used to foster meaningful prayer (a benefit to experience).

Conclusion

Jesus' teaching on prayer in Matthew 7:7–11 is so helpful, as He reinforces the value and opportunity of prayer. When we struggle with the practice of prayer, Jesus shows us how to pray. He makes talking with God accessible and achievable.

When we struggle with the desire to pray, Jesus shows us who we pray to—our heavenly Father. We are His children and can approach Him with confidence (see Gal. 4:6–7; Heb. 4:16). What a privilege prayer is!

Questions for Reflection and Discussion

1. Does prayer come easily to you? Why or why not?

2. How does the way we view prayer influence our approach to it? In your own words, why would you say prayer is important?

3. Read Matthew 7:7–8 and Matthew 6:9–13. How does Matthew 6:9–13 give you a "head start" on what to ask for?

4. Asking, seeking, and knocking are simple actions anyone can take—reminding us of the value of "simple prayer." What are some examples of "simple prayer" that come to your mind?

5. Do you tend to overcomplicate prayer, or keep it simple? Explain.

6. In Matthew 7 Jesus says, "ask and it will be given to you . . . knock and the door will be opened to you." Does this mean God will answer every prayer, exactly the way we ask it? Explain your response.

7. Make a short list of observations about the God we pray to, from Matthew 7:9–11.

8. How do these truths about God reinforce trust in Him?

9. What other truths about God (who He is and what He's done) build further trust in Him? Tie your answers to specific Scriptures as best as you can.

10. What is one way you've learned to trust God, even in the midst of prayers that didn't get answered the way you were hoping?

11. What other questions or comments do you have about anything covered in this chapter that you'd like to discuss?

12. What is your biggest takeaway from what you've discussed so far? Is there a practical step you can take to apply what you've learned?

HOW CAN I GROW AS A FOLLOWER OF JESUS?

CHAPTER 4

FASTING: EXPRESSING AN APPETITE FOR GOD

"Man shall not live on bread alone, but on every word that comes from the mouth of God." These words of Jesus in Matthew 4:4 are worth sitting in and reflecting on as we start this chapter. Let's read them again, slowly this time: "Man shall not live on bread alone, but on every word that comes from the mouth of God."

These words come in the midst of a story you may be familiar with—an encounter between Jesus and the devil just before Jesus begins His public ministry. Satan asks Jesus to turn stones into bread so Jesus can satisfy His physical hunger.

On the face of it, there doesn't seem to be anything inherently wrong with what Satan asks of Jesus here. After all, as the second person of the Trinity, Jesus is fully God and therefore *able* to turn stones to bread. Jesus is the one through whom all things are created (Col. 1:16), and in the Gospels we read accounts of Jesus demonstrating His divine power over creation—whether through multiplying loaves and fish or through calming a raging storm (see Matt. 14:13–21; 8:23–27).

As fully human ("God in the flesh," or God incarnate), Jesus' physical body needs food. In fact, Jesus' body *really* needs food here in Matthew 4. Just before Satan comes to Jesus, we read that Jesus has been in the wilderness fasting for forty days and forty nights. The end of Matthew 4:2 states Jesus' obvious reality matter-of-factly: "He was hungry."

To sum up: In His humanity, Jesus' body needs fuel. In His divinity, Jesus can make fuel—even making stones into bread. Seems like an easy decision. Right?

Not so fast.

Jesus knew there was something underneath Satan's temptation—this deceptive offer that *seemed* to have Jesus' best immediate interests in mind. Jesus knew that Satan's bait had a barb: Satan was tempting Jesus to "save Himself" on his own terms. Satan was tempting Jesus to leverage His divinity to avoid physical suffering. Satan was trying to interrupt and undermine Jesus' dependence on His heavenly Father.

Suddenly it's much clearer: The easy decision isn't always the best decision. The "quick escape" can create other long-term problems. Self-control and dependence on God—not self-centeredness or self-gratification—should be the values we champion and feed.

In Jesus' response to Satan in Mathew 4 we see a radical God-centeredness that leads to Jesus manifesting a sacrificial self-control, rather than a self-centeredness that leads to shortcuts or quick fixes. We see this radical God-centeredness in Jesus' reply: "Man shall not live on bread alone, but on every word that comes from the mouth of God" (Matt. 4:4).

This God-centeredness—and the resulting self-control it can motivate—smacks against the cultural values that sustain self-centeredness and self-gratification and that are so prevalent in our world today. Let me say what we already know: In America we prize instant gratification. You want something? You can have it that same day thanks to Amazon. Can't afford it? No problem—just swipe your credit card and increase your debt by a little bit more. Our "self-control muscle" has atrophied.

So the question we need to ask, then, is this: How can we grow in God-centeredness and the self-control this God-centeredness should motivate?

One significant piece of the answer is found in what Jesus had been doing leading up to Satan's temptations—He'd been fasting.

Fasting 101

Fasting is perhaps a discipline you're less familiar with. Donald Whitney calls Christian fasting "the most feared and misunderstood of all the Spiritual Disciplines."[23] Some have experience with fasting, but they are focused on the health or medical aspect (e.g., intermittent fasting to manage weight, or fasting from everything but water before a medical procedure). To make sure we're clear early on, the focus of this chapter is on the *spiritual* discipline of fasting—namely, how fasting helps us grow in God-centeredness and cultivate self-control.

In terms of what fasting is as a spiritual discipline, most straightforwardly it means going without food for a certain period of time in order to focus on God. (When the word *fasting* is referred to in the Bible, this definition is what's in mind.) However, fasting can also be understood more broadly as abstaining from something else other than just food. Twentieth century pastor and author D. Martyn Lloyd-Jones is helpful at expressing this broader application of fasting:

Fasting, if we conceive of it truly, must not . . . be confined to the question of food and drink; fasting should really be made to include abstinence from anything which is legitimate in and of itself for the sake of some special spiritual purpose. There are many bodily functions which are right and normal and perfectly legitimate, but which for special peculiar reasons in certain circumstances should be controlled.[24]

Understood this way, then, fasting can also include temporarily abstaining from things like social media, other forms of entertainment, sexual relations for married couples (see 1 Cor. 7:5), and more.

In terms of why fasting is important, John Mark Comer says the following: "Fasting is one of the most essential and powerful of all the practices of Jesus and, arguably, the single most neglected in the modern Western church."[25] I'll riff on Comer's statement here and add that fasting is "essential" and "powerful" for this reason: Sometimes it is necessary to say "no" to good things so we can create space for better things. In fasting, we take things that we normally depend on—most commonly food—and intentionally abstain from them to take away distractions and train ourselves in the truth that God is better. In our world today, which celebrates uncritically *filling* our appetites (we want something and so we get something), fasting helps *form* our appetites—saying no to one thing and expressing a desire for God.

Read this quote from Cornelius Plantinga slowly: "The early desert fathers believed that a person's appetites are linked: full stomachs and jaded palates take the edge from our hunger and thirst for righteousness. They spoil the appetite for God."[26] In other words, fulfilling every physical pleasure or need we have can become a distraction, "spoiling the appetite for God." It's like me telling any one of my boys why they can't have a huge snack fifteen minutes before dinner: they'll spoil their appetite for the nourishing meal that's being prepared for them.

Here's the value that the spiritual discipline of fasting adds to our formation: Temporarily denying some of our physical appetites and impulses can serve to fuel our appetite for God.

With this overview of fasting in mind, let's now dig more deeply into this discipline. In what follows, we'll explore more fully what the Bible says about fasting in a way that both (1) shows us how fasting can fuel our appetite for God, and (2) protects against possible misunderstandings or wrong approaches to this discipline.

Three Ways Fasting Can Fuel Our Appetite for God

Fasting is a fairly prominent practice mentioned throughout the Bible. (Too often we can fail to notice how often it comes up!) For example, fasting appears in every major division of the Old Testament:[27] it is mentioned in the Law (e.g., Ex. 34:28; Lev. 23:27;[28] Deut. 9:9); the Prophets (e.g., Judg. 20:26; 2 Sam. 12:16; Isa. 58; Jer. 36:9; Joel 1:14); and the Writings (e.g., Ezra 8:21; Est. 4:15–16; Ps. 35:13; 2 Chron. 20:3). Fasting is both practiced by Jesus (e.g., Matt. 4:2) and part of His teaching for His followers (e.g., Matt. 6:16–18; Luke 5:33–35). Fasting is practiced by the early church (Acts 13:2–3; 14:23).

Clearly we see that fasting is a discipline practiced by God's people. The next questions to ask, then, are "Why were they fasting?" and "How did it form them?" Spiritual disciplines are not just mindless, mechanical motions. Spiritual disciplines cultivate godliness. With this in mind, a biblical survey of fasting helps us identify key ways fasting expresses an appetite for God—included here in no particular order.[29]

First, fasting expresses **an appetite for a restored relationship with God.** The need for restoration occurs because of our sin. What I want to draw out in this point is how strongly the Bible connects the dots between fasting, repentance (or turning from sin and to God), and humility. We see this, for example, in Nehemiah 9. God's law has been read to the people in the chapter just before this (see Neh. 8:1–18). And now in Nehemiah 9, we see that part of the people's response to the truth of God's Word is awareness of sin and confession (Neh. 9:2–3). What else accompanies this awareness of sin? How does the community of God's people express repentance? Nehemiah 9:1 tells us that the people were "fasting and wearing sackcloth and putting dust on their heads."[30] Fasting was a physical expression of repentance, a display of humility and a desire to be in restored relationship with God. Donald Whitney highlights this important focus of fasting: "Fasting can represent more than just grief over sin. It also can signal a commitment to obedience and a new direction."[31] We see fasting as an expression of this repentance, desire for forgiveness, and right relationship in 1 Samuel 7:2–7, Joel 2:12, and Jonah 3:3–5 as well.

Before moving on to the next way fasting expresses an appetite for God, I need to address a question you may have as a Christian: "If Jesus has already made me right with God through His work on the cross, is fasting as an expression of repentance—for a desired restored relationship with God—no longer valuable?" Yes, followers of Jesus are made right with God entirely through faith in Jesus' finished work on the cross (see Rom. 5:1; 2 Cor. 5:21; Eph. 2:8–9). Nothing can separate us from the love of God we have through Jesus Christ (see Rom. 8:37–39). While nothing can separate us from the love of God we have through Jesus, our sin does create *relational distance* in the relationship we can have with our Lord. Just like an impatient word or prioritizing work over my marriage certainly won't *end* my relationship with my wife, these things will *affect* my relationship with Carrie—creating relational distance that I need to acknowledge and turn from. In the same way, while my sin doesn't *end* my relationship with the Lord it does *affect* my relationship with the Lord. (We must never excuse or minimize sin! For more orientation on sin, see appendix 2.) This sin needs to be repented of, and a right relationship needs to be restored. As a valuable way of expressing repentance and cultivating an appetite for restored relationship, the spiritual discipline of fasting retains a place.

Second, fasting cultivates **an appetite for God's direction.** In Acts 13:1–3, we read the following:

> Now in the church at Antioch there were prophets and teachers: Barnabas, Simeon called Niger, Lucius of Cyrene, Manaen (who had been brought up with Herod the tetrarch) and Saul. *While they were worshiping the Lord and fasting*, the Holy Spirit said, "Set apart for me Barnabas and Saul for the work to which I have called them." So after they had fasted and prayed, they placed their hands on them and sent them off. (Acts 13:1–3)

In other words, during a time of worship and fasting, the Holy Spirit "tapped Barnabas and Saul on the shoulder" and directed them toward the missionary journeys that would fill so much of the rest of the book of Acts. To be fair, we don't know that during this time of worship and fasting the early church leaders were explicitly seeking any fresh direction—that would be reading too much into the passage. *Nevertheless*, when the

Holy Spirit did direct them during this time of fasting, the church responded in straightforward obedience. Fasting, then, is certainly aligned with an openness to and appetite for receiving fresh direction from the Lord when He decides to provide it.

Third, fasting cultivates **an appetite for God's provision.** The book of Esther records the powerful story of an exiled Jewish woman (Esther) who finds herself placed in a position where she can influence a foreign king and rescue her people from destruction. Esther's actions take courage and leadership; Esther knows any success depends on the Lord. In Esther 4—just before Esther boldly approaches the king at great potential cost to herself—she reaches out to her cousin, Mordecai. Notice what Esther asks for:

> Go, gather together all the Jews who are in Susa, and fast for me. Do not eat or drink for three days, night or day. I and my attendants will fast as you do. When this is done, I will go to the king, even though it is against the law. And if I perish, I perish. (Est. 4:16)

Esther knows she needs God to work on her behalf, and so she asks for a fast. Surely this fast is directed toward dependence on God to provide any number of things: courage for Esther, a favorable outcome to her request of the king, and a God-centeredness that will fuel Esther's bold steps.

We see fasting connected to God's provision also in Ezra 8. As God's people return to Jerusalem from exile, Ezra proclaims a fast, asking God to provide a safe journey (Ezra 8:21, 23). Second Samuel 12:16, 2 Chronicles 20:1–4, Nehemiah 1:4, Psalm 109:24–26, and Acts 14:23 provide additional glimpses of fasting that are connected to dependence on God's provision.

The broader takeaway from this biblical survey is that the spiritual discipline of fasting expresses an appetite for God's presence and activity. This appetite for God's presence and activity demands humility on our part. It requires an acknowledgment of our dependence on God and an appreciation for His glorious, powerful character. It assumes a readiness to respond and act on who God is and how He guides.

Three Misunderstandings About Fasting

A survey of what the Bible says about fasting doesn't only reveal how this discipline can cultivate an appetite for God's presence and activity; Scripture also alerts us to ways that fasting can be misunderstood.

One such misunderstanding is that **fasting is a formula:** go through the motions and that's enough. Isaiah 58 corrects this misunderstanding. In Isaiah 58, the people are fasting all right (Isa. 58:3–4). But despite the mechanical motions of fasting, they are forsaking God's commands (Isa. 58:2)—showing both their distance from God and their neglect of their neighbor. We see this neglect, for example, in their exploitation of others, overlooking of oppression, and lack of care for the poor and hungry (Isa. 58:4–7). This neglect of others is fueled by the people's selfishness (Isa. 58:13) and has created distance from God. But if people turn from their selfishness and care for the needy in their midst, God offers His own guidance, provision, and joy (Isa. 58:11, 14).

In other words, to experience these amazing realities of God's presence and activity, fasting-as-a-formula isn't sufficient. *Fasting is not a formula.* It's not a silver bullet. Going through the motions isn't enough. We need personal holiness and love for neighbor. To say it again: The qualities that invite God's blessing here in Isaiah 58 are God-centeredness, humility, and others-centeredness (see also Matt. 22:37–40). When fasting is added to these essential qualities, fasting finds its best expression. When fasting is divorced from these qualities— when fasting is misunderstood as only a going-through-the-motions formula—the discipline falls flat and can feed spiritual misunderstanding or even damage.

Another related misunderstanding of fasting is that **motives don't matter.** Rather, *motives do matter* as Jesus so clearly teaches in His Sermon on the Mount:

> When you fast, do not look somber as the hypocrites do, for they disfigure their faces to show others they are fasting. Truly I tell you, they have received their reward in full. But when you fast, put oil on your head and wash your face, so that it will not be obvious to others that you are fasting, but only to your Father, who is unseen; and your Father, who sees what is done in secret, will reward you. (Matt. 6:16–18)

Don't miss that Jesus says *"when* you fast . . ."" Jesus underscores the importance of this spiritual discipline! But He also helps us assess our motives. Fasting should not be done to draw attention to yourself. Fasting should not be done to spotlight your supposed spiritual maturity. Fasting is about focusing your attention on God and your desperate need for Him; we must be careful to align our motives with this focus of fasting.

I'll mention one more misunderstanding of fasting that Scripture helps us see—what I'll call **an infatuation with fasting**. In 1 Timothy 4:1-5, Paul warns Timothy about false and deceptive teaching, part of which includes ordering people to "abstain from certain foods" (1 Tim. 4:3). For these false teachers, fasting seemed to be a mandate for spiritual maturity rather than a meaningful discipline that can cultivate maturity. The focus was so much on "going without" that these false teachers overlooked the good things (including food!) that we can enjoy and receive with thanksgiving (1 Tim. 4:3–4). So while fasting has its place, at the same time fasting must be kept in place—an important discipline to be sure, but not *the* measuring stick for spiritual maturity.

Fasting: Tools for the Toolbox

With this biblical survey in mind—knowing both how to approach fasting biblically and what misunderstandings to avoid—how can we pursue this spiritual discipline, practically speaking? Here are two areas that are worth attention as you consider practical application—these can prime the pump for your own thinking as you apply what you've learned in this chapter.

First, consider the type of fast you want to pursue. By far the most common type of fast is abstaining from food for a set amount of time—perhaps for a meal, or a day, or a weekend for example. Until you've done further study on fasting and consult with a medical doctor, you should still drink plenty of water during this time. Many people modify this slightly to also include drinking natural fruit or vegetable juices during their fast. (Energy drinks, caffeine, and other drinks high in sugar are generally discouraged during this fast from food.)

Another type of fast is really a subset of fasting from food. This second type of fast is often called a "Daniel fast," loosely following the model of Daniel and his friends in Daniel 1. There we read that Daniel "resolved not to defile himself with the royal food and wine" (Dan. 1:8). They didn't abstain from food entirely, however. Rather, they ate only vegetables and drank only water (see Dan. 1:12). While this isn't a prescriptive passage—that is, this passage isn't issuing commands or examples that the people of God are required to follow—this example does lead some to periodically adopt this "Daniel fast," which is essentially a restricted diet of simple, natural foods.

Yet another type of fast is abstaining from otherwise good or neutral practices for a time—such as social media, watching television, etc.—to rein in our habits, exercise self-control, and prioritize time in more decidedly godly pursuits. As you consider types of fasting, a final consideration to keep in mind is whether the fast will be an individual fast (what Jesus is doing in Matthew 4) or a group fast (e.g., Acts 13:1–2). A group fast can be as small as two to three other believers, or it can include a larger group (e.g., your small group or church family).

Second, give thought to the *before*, *during*, and *after* of the fast you have in mind. Once you have decided what type of fast you'll be practicing, I encourage you to have a simple plan for the fast. Remember, the spiritual discipline of fasting is more than forgetting to eat or skipping a meal for any reason that may be related to physical health. Fasting expresses an appetite for God, and this purpose should be clear in the fast itself.

Before the fast, then, you'll want to have a clear idea of what type of fasting you'll be doing. Review the section above on "ways fasting can cultivate an appetite for God" and prayerfully consider whether anything in that section provides additional focus to your fast or whether your fast will be broader—a more general expression of desire for God and His activity.

The length of your fast is another question to answer before you fast. If you're fasting from food, I encourage people to start with fasting for one to three meals before you jump into anything significantly longer than that. (This is especially true if you've never fasted before or if fasting has not been a regular rhythm in your life.)

As you plan your fast on the front end, you'll also want to have a simple plan for how you'll spend the time actually fasting. The spiritual discipline of fasting isn't getting an extra sixty minutes of work in because you're skipping lunch. It's filling the time you would have spent eating (or watching television, etc.) with prayer and Bible reading, for example. To facilitate clarity about this plan for how you'll spend your fast, I recommend very briefly answering these questions:

1. What am I fasting *from* (e.g., food, "evening unwind" TV)?

2. How will I spend that time instead (e.g., prayer, journaling, Bible reading)?

3. How long will this fast be (e.g., one meal, one day, one weekend)?

Answering these simple questions with very brief responses should culminate in clarity. For example:

- I'm fasting from (1) <u>lunch and supper this Monday</u> [what you're fasting from] to focus instead on (2) <u>extended Bible reading and prayer</u> [how you'll spend the time instead]. I plan to do this for (3) <u>one day</u> [how long the fast will be].

- I'm fasting from (1) <u>social media</u> [what you're fasting from] to focus instead on (2) <u>cultivating rhythms of structured prayer in my life</u> [how you'll spend the time instead]. I plan to do this for (3) <u>ten days</u> [how long the fast will be].

- I'm fasting from (1) <u>my lunchtime meal on Wednesdays</u> [what you're fasting from] to focus instead on (2) <u>praying for my neighbors who don't know the Lord</u> [how you'll spend the time instead]. I plan to do this for (3) <u>one semester</u> [how long the fast will be].

These are *examples* intended to give you a picture of what intentional fasting can look like. My hope is that these examples spark your own thinking about what the spiritual discipline of fasting can look like in your own life.

One more thought pertaining to planning the fast, before you fast: With this plan in place that you've been talking about, you may need to block off time in your schedule in order to have lunches free (if you're planning on fasting every Wednesday for a semester, for example). You may want to think about the physical environment you're in during your times of extended Bible reading and prayer—an environment free from distraction as much as possible and where others know not to call unless it's an emergency.

If you've been intentional with some simple planning, your time *during the fast* now has focus and space. Now, during the fast, is the time to implement the plan you've prayerfully considered and to benefit from this time with God that is punctuated by some physical self-denial—an expression of your greater appetite for Him.

Other chapters in this book dive more deeply into some of the positive spiritual disciplines to which you devote time during your fast (e.g., engaging the Bible, extended time in prayer, etc.). I won't revisit those here, though I encourage you to review those chapters if doing so would serve how you spend your time fasting. Here I simply want to highlight three cautions to watch out for while you're fasting.

First, don't fast to draw attention to yourself (see Matt. 6:16–18). Remember, fasting is an expression of our appetite for God. If you're wanting attention, appreciation, or accolades for your fast, your motives need to be checked, repented of, and redirected. Importantly, what Jesus says in Matthew 6:16–18 doesn't mean you can't participate in group fasts! (I've had some people ask whether *anyone* knowing we're fasting—even others who are part of a group fast—disobeys Jesus' teaching there.) What Jesus is getting at in Matthew 6 is the driving motive for our fast. He is warning us against fasting to draw attention to ourselves. While we can fast alongside others (there are so many group fasts in the Bible!), we should not fast to be seen by others. The issue is motive for fasting, not the number of people involved in a fast.

Second, don't get frustrated if things don't go exactly according to your plan. A plan for fasting can provide healthy direction, but your plan shouldn't be a straitjacket that allows for zero wiggle room. God is a personal Actor who may redirect you during your fast in a significant way (see Acts 13:1–2). There could be a situation where your fast is interrupted by a well-intentioned person who wants to engage in conversation, or by an emergency that needs immediate attention. In any of these conceivable scenarios, our response shouldn't be frustration. If fasting truly is an expression of self-denial, we need to know that at times *my* plan for *my* fast done *my* way is best served by those plans being redirected. Since fasting is a way to cultivate godliness, our response to these interruptions should manifest the fruit of the Spirit (Gal. 5:22–23) and not frustration.

During the fast—even while we follow the broad contours of the plan we have prayerfully established—we should keep our eyes and hearts open to the ways God Himself may step in and work. God can absolutely work through our plans. But He won't always.

A third warning is more of a practical heads-up: Many experience headaches or hunger pangs during the first few hours of their fast. Knowing to expect these physical effects can help you persevere through them, and they provide a tangible reminder to depend on God. If physical symptoms worsen or persist, consult a medical professional or consider ending the fast early.

Let's now very briefly talk about reflecting on the fast, *after the fast*. Your set time of fasting is finished. What now? First— and very tactically—don't swing to the other end of the pendulum after your fast. If you've been fasting from food, don't gorge yourself for the next week, using your fast as an excuse for gluttony. If you've been fasting from social media, don't hop back on your platform of choice and doomscroll for three hours to catch up on everything you missed. While we can enjoy food and even technology (see 1 Tim. 4:4; 6:17), we must be careful not to retreat back to any of these for the soul-level satisfaction we find only in Jesus (Phil. 3:7–11). I talked with one friend who mentioned intentionally planning the time of their fast so that they would end their fast with taking the Lord's Supper at church.[32]

Second, journal takeaways or conclusions from your fasting. However the fast went—good or bad, easy or difficult—what are three to five takeaways from that time fasting? These takeaways can be lessons you want to carry forward into your life, insights from God's Word that you need to reflect on further, or practical tips for how to continue making the most of future fasts.

Conclusion

Let's end where we began this chapter: "Man does not live by bread alone" (Matt. 4:4).

Our greatest desire should not be for food or having our physical appetites satisfied. Our greatest desire should be to know God and center our lives around Him. How can we express this appetite for God? Fasting deserves a place in our toolbox of Christian formation—denying ourselves, looking to God, and being formed into Christ's likeness.

Questions for Reflection and Discussion

1. The Bible mentions fasting (purposefully going without food for a period of time) as a spiritual discipline. What comes to your mind first when you think about fasting? What questions do you have about it? Do you have any personal experience with fasting?

2. Notice that Jesus says *"when* you fast . . ."* in Matthew 6:16–17. (He doesn't say *if* you fast.) Why is fasting important as followers of Jesus? (Hint: see also Matthew 4:4.)

3. What approach to fasting is Jesus discouraging in Matthew 6:16? What might this look like today?

4. How can fasting cultivate an "appetite for God"?

5. While fasting in the Bible refers to abstaining from food for a time, followers of Jesus may sometimes also choose to abstain from other good things as a way to cultivate their appetite for God. Make a list of other things (even things that are otherwise good) that can distract our attention away from God, such that a periodic "fast" from these things may be worth considering. (Example: social media.)

6. Fasting isn't only going without. It's also "filling up" with other things like prayer, Bible reading, and worship. Why is it important to include this "filling up" emphasis as well?

7. What practical considerations should be taken into consideration regarding fasting? Why are these important to keep in mind?

8. What other questions or comments do you have about anything covered in this chapter that you'd like to discuss?

9. What is your biggest takeaway from what you've discussed so far? Is there a practical step you can take to apply what you've learned?

HOW CAN I GROW AS A FOLLOWER OF JESUS?

CHAPTER 5
SOLITUDE & SILENCE: CROWDING OUR
LIVES WITH GOD

"Busy."

Ask me how I'm doing in passing and—more likely than not—this one word, "busy," will be the response I give you. I'll usually follow it up with something like "*good busy*, though—which is better than the alternative."

The reality though (which I don't really think about when I'm in the moment) is that when I respond with "busy," I'm not even answering the question about how I'm doing at all. Am I frustrated or fulfilled? Do I feel chaotic on the inside, or content? I can be busy and frustrated, or I can be busy and fulfilled. I can be busy and chaotic, or busy and content. "Busy" *sounds* good (after all, if you're busy you must be busy doing something important, right?). But "busyness" can become the easy answer, a smoke screen that keeps me from lingering too long on how I'm doing, *really*.

As we seek to grow in Christlikeness as Jesus' disciples, we need to discern who we actually are beneath the surface of events and externals. So whether we're experiencing busyness, suffering, success, or any number of other things—we discern if we're modeling the fruit of the Spirit or the deeds of the flesh (Gal. 5:19–23), the wisdom of the world or the wisdom from above (James 3:13–18).

So the question is, How can we discern who we actually are beneath the surface of our lives? How can we rise above the events and externals and see ourselves a little more clearly? Like with most things, the answer is multifaceted: We need the truth of God's Word, the work of God's Spirit, and the wisdom of God's people. All of these are important.

There's also another important ingredient in seeing ourselves clearly, discerning who we are beneath the surface of our lives: the discipline of silence and solitude. Writing in the seventeenth century, John Owen penned words that echo across the centuries with force still today: "What we are in [our times of solitude], that we are indeed, and no more. They are either the best or the worst of our times, wherein the principle that is predominant in us will show and act itself."[33]

Solitude clears away other noise so there's nothing else to distract us from the sound and inclinations of our own heart. Solitude and silence help us see ourselves more clearly.

This discipline will be the focus of this chapter. (Note to the reader: I consider solitude and silence as most often belonging together. For simplicity's sake I will reference them together as "solitude" in this chapter.)

SOLITUDE AS A WAY OF SEEING YOURSELF CLEARLY

How does solitude help us see ourselves clearly? Peter Kreeft is helpful here:

> We *want* to complexify our lives. We don't have to, we *want* to. We want to be harried and hassled and busy. Unconsciously, we want the very things we complain about. For if we had leisure [think: space, margin], we would look at ourselves and listen to our hearts and see the great gaping hole in our hearts and be terrified, because that hole is so big that nothing but God can fill it.[34]

This quote unsettles me. It unsettles me because of all the ways I can relate to it. I complexify my life. I feel harried and hassled and busy. I complain about being busy and then in the very next breath schedule something else on my calendar. I fill my life with noise and distractions that keep me from listening to my heart. Becoming a Chistian doesn't immediately change any of these tendencies that are endemic to our lives. Even when we've surrendered our lives to God and placed our faith in Christ as followers of Jesus, we can so easily fill our time with distractions that numb us to how we're doing and deflect us from who we're becoming.

But this Peter Kreeft quote doesn't only unsettle me. It also points me forward. Kreeft mentions leisure time. By "leisure time" he's not talking about time to unwind while you're bingeing a show and scrolling on your phone at the same time. This "leisure time" isn't working out at the gym with earbuds in all the while. (To be clear: "Unwinding" in the evening or listening to a podcast while you exercise of course aren't bad things. But when examples like this are our *only* category for leisure, our view is skewed.) The "leisure time" Kreeft mentions is space to reflect. Space with plenty of unrushed margin for you to think deeply and give devoted attention to things that matter most—"listening to our hearts" as Kreeft says.

This space to reflect and listen to our hearts is largely what I have in mind with the discipline of solitude and silence. The only further nuance I'd add—just to make sure things are clear in our age that elevates self as ultimate—is that it's space to reflect and listen to our hearts *in light of God*. "Listening to our hearts" is not about inflating a view of self but about orienting a view of self around God. Solitude isn't only about looking within; even more importantly it's about intentional time to look *up*, considering our lives before God.

So with all that in mind, the definition of solitude I'll work from in this chapter is this: In solitude we intentionally pull *away from* other commitments and clear away any potential distractions so we can *enter into* an uncrowded, uninterrupted space, *for the purposes of* reflection and listening in light of God.

Solitude Throughout Scripture: A Sampling

As we root this discipline in Scripture, the clearest and strongest case for solitude can be seen in the commitment of Jesus Himself to this practice. Early in the gospel of Mark, we read of Jesus' very active ministry life. He's teaching in the synagogue (Mark 1:22) and healing many others late into the evening—perhaps even early into the next morning (Mark 1:32–34). Sounds like a good reason for Jesus to sleep in the next morning, right? But that's not what we read. Immediately after Jesus' full day and late night, Mark 1:35 tells us "*Very early in the morning, while it was still dark*, Jesus got up, left the house and went off to a solitary place, where he prayed."

Jesus prioritized solitude enough to sacrifice some sleep and begin His day away from others in prayer to God.

This example from Mark 1 is by no means an exception in the life of Jesus. Throughout the Gospels, we read again and again of Jesus practicing solitude. In his *Celebration of Discipline*, Richard Foster has compiled many such mentions of Jesus prioritizing solitude at key points in His earthly ministry:

> [Jesus] inaugurated his ministry by spending forty days alone in the dessert (Matt. 4:1–11). Before he chose the twelve he spent the entire night alone in the desert hills (Luke 6:12). When he received news of John the Baptist's death, he 'withdrew from there in a boat to a lonely place apart' (Matt. 14:13). After the miraculous feeding of the five thousand Jesus 'went up into the hills by himself . . .' (Matt. 14:23). Following a long night of work, 'in the morning, a great while before day, he rose and went out to a lonely place . . .' (Mark 1:35). When the twelve returned from a preaching and healing mission, Jesus instructed them, 'Come away by yourselves to a lonely place' (Mark 6:31). Following the healing of a leper Jesus 'withdrew to the wilderness and prayed' (Luke 5:16). With three disciples he sought out the silence of a lonely mountain as the stage for the transfiguration (Matt. 17:1–9). As he prepared for his highest and most holy work, Jesus sought the solitude of the garden of Gethsemane (Matt. 26:36–46).[35]

Author John Mark Comer helpfully points out that solitude didn't only coincide with the "highlight reel" of Jesus' ministry. "On the night before his arrest, Jesus went to Gethsemane, a park outside the city of Jerusalem. [A great place to find solitude!] The writer Luke tells us he went there 'as usual.' . . . For Jesus, the secret place [i.e., the place of solitude] wasn't just a place, it was a *practice*, a habit, a part of his life rhythm."[36]

Now back to Foster to drive things home: "the seeking out of solitary places was a regular practice for Jesus. So it should be for us."[37]

While the value and priority of solitude are clear in the life of Jesus, the Gospels are not the only place in Scripture that we learn of the formative power of solitude in the lives of others.

Consider the life of Moses. Though born an Israelite at a time when the lives of Israelite male babies were at risk, Moses' life is miraculously spared and he's raised by Pharoah's daughter in the Egyptian court (see Ex. 1:1–2:10; Acts 7:21–22). Exodus 2:11–3:6 then recounts how the adult Moses murders an Egyptian who is beating an Israelite, which in turn propels Moses to flee the court of Egypt out of fear for his life (Ex. 2:15). Moses ends up in the land of Midian where he lives the life of a shepherd.

Enter: Solitude.

Imagine being Moses and going from the constant hustle and bustle of crowds in the Egyptian court to the life of a shepherd—long stretches of time (perhaps entire days, or even a long string of days) without seeing another person in the Midian wilderness. This new reality wasn't just for a few days or a few weeks. Moses lived as a shepherd in Midian for *forty years* (see Acts 7:29–30). And then, after forty years of this life, God visits Moses in the burning bush and sends him to deliver the Israelites from slavery (Ex. 3:1–10).

How did these forty years of solitude shape Moses? We don't fully know. I want to resist fanciful speculation and trying to psychoanalyze Moses millennia after he walked the earth. At the same time, the Bible does provide some clues and glimpses.

In Exodus 2, it seems that Moses killed the Egyptian as a way to take matters into his own hands—to exact justice when justice was absent. And yet in Exodus 3 when God calls Moses to deliver the Israelites from slavery (remember: this is forty years after he fled Egypt), Moses doesn't want his hands anywhere in that situation as he makes excuse after excuse for why he shouldn't go—with Moses' first excuse being "who am I?" (see Ex. 3:11). Moses has gone from being the one who steps in to take matters into his own hands, to a much lower estimation of himself. He's gone from savior complex to seeing that without God he's powerless. The time in the desert—time in solitude—had formed Moses.

In Hebrews 11, we get one more glimpse into how Moses' time in solitude shaped him:

> By faith Moses, when he had grown up, refused to be known as the son of Pharaoh's daughter. He chose to be mistreated along with the people of God rather than to enjoy the fleeting pleasures of sin. He regarded disgrace for the sake of Christ as of greater value than the treasures of Egypt, because he was looking ahead to his reward. By faith he left Egypt, not fearing the king's anger; he persevered because he saw him who is invisible. (Heb. 11:24–27)

It seems to be that these four verses summarize decades of Moses' life. Hebrews commentator Gareth Lee Cockerill identifies Moses' refusal "to be known as the son of Pharaoh's daughter" (Heb. 11:24) with Moses' killing of the Egyptian slave master, before Moses' flight to Midian.[38] But then Cockerill seems to focus much of his discussion regarding Moses' mistreatment and suffering of disgrace (Heb. 11:25–26) *after* Moses' wilderness (i.e., solitude) experience in Midian, upon Moses' return to free the Israelites.[39]

In other words, verses 24 and 25 in Hebrews 11 span approximately forty years. What happened *in* Moses during these forty years? Whatever else may be part of an answer, this time of relative solitude shaped Moses' desires in such a way that the fleeting pleasures of sin and the treasures of Egypt had no hold on him; He had encountered God Himself ("he saw him who is invisible," Heb. 11:27) and was singularly focused on pleasing God. Moses' encountering God in solitude transformed Moses' desires and prepared him for what was ahead.

What we can say for sure is that Moses died a godly man: standing out for his humility (Num. 12:3) and included in the "faith hall of fame" of Hebrews 11. However it happened precisely and whatever exact effect it had, Moses' forty years of solitude were part of the shaping influence that led to his humility and faith (see Rom. 8:28). Solitude was a shaping influence in the life of Moses.

Or very briefly, consider also the life of Paul. Paul was a man on the move: planting churches and encouraging disciples all throughout the Mediterranean world (e.g., Acts 14:21–25; Rom. 15:20, 23–28). Yet there were times when Paul was forced to slow down in his many imprisonments. (Importantly, Paul didn't find joy *in* the solitude of imprisonment. Rather, *through* the solitude of imprisonment God worked in and through Paul in key ways.) These times of "forced solitude" allowed Paul the space to write numerous New Testament letters—Ephesians, Philippians, Colossians, and Philemon are often called the "prison epistles" because of the commonly held view that these letters were written while Paul was imprisoned.[40] Paul's "forced solitude" helped him learn more of the sufficiency of Christ and true contentment (Phil. 4:11–

13; see also 2 Tim. 4:16–18). Paul's forced solitude provided fresh insights into the nature of Christian joy (e.g., Phil. 1:18–20; see also Rom. 5:3–5). Solitude was a shaping influence in the life of Paul.

From this introductory survey of Scripture, we can start to draw together some conclusions about solitude we don't want to miss. One the one hand, there are times we see that solitude is sought. We see this most notably in the life of Jesus. On the other hand, sometimes solitude is involuntary—Moses' unplanned flight to Midian, and Paul's time in prison. While the practical helps for solitude this chapter will outline are most focused on "voluntary" solitude—the solitude we can seek out and plan—we must not overlook the formative power of solitude that is thrust upon us in any number of ways, for any number of reasons.

Regardless of whether the solitude we experience is voluntarily pursued or involuntarily thrust upon us, solitude can form us in relationship with God.

Solitude: Tools for the Toolbox

Solitude *can* form us in relationship with God, but it may not. Solitude can frustrate us, if our expectations for that time aren't met. Or solitude can instead frighten us, as it exposes more of who we are and what lies beneath the surface of our lives when distractions are quieted: "Solitude is a terrible trial, for it serves to crack open and burst apart the shell of our superficial securities. It opens out to us the unknown abyss that we all carry within us . . . [and] discloses the fact that these abysses are haunted."[41]

The question then becomes: How can we approach solitude in a way that helps us get the most out of this discipline? Below

I've included three keys that can help you unlock benefits from solitude.

One key to maximize the practice of solitude is to keep in mind that this discipline is what I call a "secondary discipline." By "secondary" I don't mean in any way that its importance is diminished (our biblical survey has shown us how vital this discipline is!); rather, I mean this discipline doesn't stand alone, apart from other disciplines we've already explored. To say it positively: I believe solitude is best practiced alongside other disciplines like biblical meditation and prayer.

To return to the working definition of solitude we're using in this chapter: In solitude we intentionally pull *away from* other commitments and clear away any potential distractions so we can *enter into* an uncrowded, uninterrupted space, *for the purposes of* reflection and listening in light of God. We must not truncate this definition to say solitude is "pulling away from other commitments and clearing away any potential distractions so we can enter into an uncrowded, uninterrupted space [full stop]." We must include the final phrase: "*for the purposes of* reflection and listening in light of God." We must not separate the presence of God from the practice of solitude.

So how best do we reflect and listen, in light of God? The answer is so straightforward we may miss it: Scripture and prayer. While I don't need to repeat things I've already mentioned in earlier chapters on these topics, I will at minimum encourage bringing along a Bible with you while you practice times of extended solitude, or having a small handful of verses on which you want to meditate more deeply. I encourage you to bring a pen and a journal so you can write out prayers and capture thoughts you have during your solitude. Knowing how distracting digital devices can be, I encourage you to bring along a physical Bible, and a physical journal if at all possible— rather than relying on apps on your phone.

Another key to being formed through solitude is to make use of the small times we all have in our day. Once upon a time, a commute to work would have included stretches of silence, waiting in line at the store or the bank could have given you opportunity to reflect on something you were learning, or drifting off to sleep would have provided the chance to review the day. Now, however, commutes are filled with music or a podcast, waiting in line means scrolling through your phone, and we often fall asleep to whatever streaming platform we're watching to unwind. Even the thirty seconds we're waiting at stoplights are too often filled with checking our phones!

The point I'm trying to make is that you have small times in your day where you can practice the discipline of solitude and silence. Still don't believe me? Take out your phone right now and check your "screen time" usage for social and entertainment apps. If you're like me, you'll be surprised at how much time sneaks away into our phones! Repurposing these small times for solitude or silence just takes a little forethought and intentionality. Can you leave your radio off when you're driving to work or school? Can you make a commitment to not check your phone when you're in line at the grocery store? What can you shift around in your life so you have space to review a memory verse, mediate on who God is, or reflect on how He's worked in your day before you drift off to sleep?

A third key to maximize the benefits that solitude offers is to plan extended times of solitude throughout your year. These "extended times of solitude" are more than the 20–30 minutes you may spend doing daily devotions. As vital as that daily time is, these extended times of solitude that I have in mind start at two to three hours of solitude, and go up from there. There's nothing magic or super spiritual about two to three hours as the base of this "extended" timeframe. In my experience, it's just long enough for people to feel the stretch that the practice of solitude brings. And, frankly, it's doable. It means replacing one movie or sporting event with this practice of solitude. I know many that take longer periods of time: an entire afternoon, an entire day, or even a stretch of two to three days to devote to solitude—anywhere from one to four times per year.

Once a time for this extended solitude is set, it can be helpful to think in terms of three stages: (1) preparation for the time of solitude, (2) the actual time of solitude itself, and (3) capturing takeaways after the time of solitude.

In terms of preparation, you'll want to have answers to three questions. First, *Where are you going to go?* Plan on finding a secluded space free from distraction. For many people, nature or a library is good. A spot in your home can work, as long as you won't be bombarded by distractions or your to-do list.

Second, *How will you "protect" your time and space? Have you made appropriate arrangements?* This includes alerting appropriate people that you'll be out of touch for a few hours, and setting "focus" features on your devices so you won't be getting alerts and notifications. Be sure to let those closest to you know where you'll be and how you can be reached in case of emergency; this is especially true if you'll be taking a time of solitude for longer than two to three hours.

Third, *What are you going to bring?* Certainly plan for the environment you'll be in (hint: don't forget bug spray if you'll be outside in nature!). Determine what else you'll need to bring for this time: items like a Bible, journal and pen, a hymnal or song sheets, and earbuds if you want to listen to worship music. Decide beforehand what you'll leave behind: your phone, other electronics, or anything else that could easily be a distraction for you.

In terms of the actual time of solitude itself, I often encourage knowing how you want to fill the first hour or so, but then intentionally *not* planning it out too much from there.

When I've led others in times of extended solitude in the past, there have been times I've had them start in a passage of Scripture (e.g., Psalm 16, John 15, or Colossians 3), journal their thoughts about the passage, and then have that launch them in a time of prayer, reflection, and examination.

Another idea for using the actual time of solitude is to plan in terms of four simple, very loosely structured steps. **Step one is "release"**—begin by writing down how you're coming into this time of solitude. For example: How do you feel? What's big or overwhelming in your life? Turn these things over to God and entrust this time to Him.

Step two is "examine." Look at your life. What do you need to confess? What needs to happen in you to orient you toward God in this time of solitude?

Step three is "receive." Spend time in Scripture, slowly and prayerfully/meditatively engaging with God's Word.

And finally, **step four is "attend."** Simply "attend" to what you've seen in God's Word—an intentionally broad category. Rather than moving on from God's Word, the time of solitude gives space to sit in it and let its truth shape who we're becoming. Commune with Him in light of who He is and what He's done.

In terms of the third stage of solitude—capturing takeaways—I encourage people to set aside the final 20–30 minutes of their time to identify both (1) ways this practice of solitude has been formative in itself, and (2) how they can carry lessons forward into their life of engagement in the world and their normal rhythms of life. As a simple guide for this takeaway reflection, below I've included a series of questions that flow out of the 6C Picture of Discipleship[42] (growing holistically in Christlikeness)—helping you consider how this time of solitude has formed you, and/or how you can carry forward what you've learned.

Two quick words about these questions: First, you may not have clear answers in every category. I encourage people to reflect on three to four of these categories, if they don't feel like they're able to respond to all six.

Second, these questions are designed to get people thinking about ways they've been formed and how they can carry takeaways forward. If other questions or exercises serve this purpose, you should not feel restricted to only these questions.

- **Commitment:** How has anything about this time in solitude stirred or refreshed my personal commitment to God?

- **Communion with God:** How have I experienced friendship or relationship with the triune God during this time of solitude? What truths about who God is can help you relate to Him faithfully? Are there ways the truths of the gospel became fresh or vivid?

- **Community with others:** What have I learned that I need to carry forward into the ways I relate to others? Are there specific relationships to which I need to apply these lessons?

- **Character:** Has this time in solitude exposed parts of my character that need attention? Has this time in solitude awakened me to character traits I need to grow in?

- **Conduct:** Has this time in solitude exposed parts of my conduct that need attention? Has this time in solitude awakened me to areas of conduct I need to grow in?

- **Commission:** What can I carry forward into service of others? What can I share from this time of solitude, with a non-Christian I'm in relationship with?

Conclusion

At the beginning of this chapter, I made the claim that solitude helps us see ourselves more clearly. But we must not forget what so much of this chapter has emphasized: the spiritual discipline of solitude must be exercised "in light of God." Solitude apart from God helps us see who we are, and that's it. If left here, we feel discouraged, vulnerable, and exposed. Solitude in light of God offers direction, hope, and grace—helping us see who we are in His sight, who we should be, who we can be.

Solitude creates opportunity to linger in the verbs of 2 Corinthians 3:18: "And we all, who with unveiled faces contemplate the Lord's glory, are being transformed into his image with ever-increasing glory, which comes from the Lord, who is the Spirit." As we contemplate the Lord's glory[43]—the person and work of Christ that we read about in the Gospels, and the One that the whole Bible is ultimately about (John 5:39)—as we contemplate the Lord's glory, we're transformed.

The action we can take in this verse is the step of contemplation, and contemplation can't be rushed. Solitude carves out space for unrushed contemplation—reflecting and listening in light of God—in a way that increasingly transforms us into Christlikeness.

Solitude in light of God helps us see who we are, who we should be, and—by God's amazing grace—who we can be.

_____

Questions for Reflection and Discussion

1. In your own words, share why the discipline of solitude is important to cultivate.

2. Does the idea of solitude and silence for an extended period of time excite you or intimidate you? Why?

3. This chapter emphasized the importance of solitude *in light of God*. Summarize what this phrase *in light of God* means, in your own words.

4. How does seeing solitude as uncrowded time with God distinguish it from pure isolation? Why is this important to keep in mind?

5. What obstacles *from our larger culture* get in the way of practicing solitude? List as many external obstacles (or distractions) as you can think of.

6. What can you do to overcome these obstacles *around* you?

7. Alongside these external obstacles to solitude (obstacles from our culture), are there still internal obstacles to overcome? What are some examples of "internal obstacles"?

8. What can you do to overcome these obstacles *within* you?

9. What is one "baby step" you can take to explore the practice of solitude in your life this week—practicing solitude in 5- to 15-minute periods?

10. What other questions or comments do you have about anything covered in this chapter that you'd like to discuss?

11. What is your biggest takeaway from what you've discussed so far? Is there a practical step you can take to apply what you've learned?

CHAPTER 6

APPRECIATING THE CHURCH: THE ROLE OF THE CHURCH IN SPIRITUAL FORMATION

Every year or two, I watch the *Band of Brothers*—a ten-part miniseries produced in 2001 that follows the story of the paratroop Easy Company through World War II. The series won all sorts of awards and remains tremendously popular: In 2019—almost two decades after the *Band of Brothers* was first released—the British newspaper *The Guardian* ranked the show #68 on its list of the 100 best TV shows of the twenty-first century.[44]

Throughout the series, the episodes include interview vignettes with the actual men depicted by characters in the show. One of these main characters is Captain Richard Winters, and during one of the interviews with the real-life Winters, he shares a question his grandson asked him: "Grandpa, were you a hero in the war?"

Quick time-out: As viewers of the show, we know Winters was a hero. His discipline, care, courage, and command come out again and again. But in the interview as he answers this question, Winters doesn't think about any of that. His eyes aren't on himself.

Back to the question: "Grandpa, were you a hero in the war?"

As Winters answers he chokes up. You can feel his emotion here. Here's how Winters does answer: "No. But I served in a company of heroes."[45]

This response by Richard Winters challenges the me-first (or me-only) mentality that permeates so much of the water we swim in today. Winters understood that he was part of something bigger than himself. He understood that we can do greater things together than we can on our own. Together we can be greater than we are as isolated individuals.

As we answer the question we're addressing in this book, ("How can I grow as a follower of Jesus?"), this perspective of community—we need others, and others need us—is one we can't overlook.

To fully answer the question, we need to zoom out a bit— past the circle we stand in. Yes, we need personal ownership and the practice of individual disciplines. (We focused on these disciplines earlier in the book.) *We also need each other and what we can do together.* We need the church. Not "church" as in a building but "church" as in the people of God, doing what the people of God are called to do. Christian growth doesn't only involve *me*, it's also about *we*.

We need to understand what Richard Winters highlighted in the quote I mentioned earlier: we're part of something bigger than ourselves. In this chapter I want to show you from the Bible that following Jesus as His disciple includes practices that go beyond "you and Jesus." Following Jesus is personal, but it is not private.[46]

We need a view of discipleship large enough that it *necessarily* includes the church.

Connecting Matthew 28 to Acts 2

In just a minute we'll slow down in Acts 2 so you see the value of community for discipleship, and then we're going to focus on three priorities that are essential ingredients for a corporate life of discipleship. But first I want to anchor what we're talking about in Matthew 28:19–20, a passage we must never get too far away from as we talk about discipleship (it's that important):

> Therefore go and make disciples of all nations, baptizing them in the name of the Father and of the Son and of the Holy Spirit, and teaching them to obey everything I have commanded you. And surely I am with you always, to the very end of the age. (Matt. 28:19–20)

These are Jesus' final words in Matthew, so we know they're important. This Great Commission of Jesus is what drives the mission of the church still today. This is the same mission that drove the earliest church, as the apostles and early disciples carried Jesus' words forward in the days and weeks after His ascension.

So the question I want to ask us, then, is this: How did the earliest church make disciples? With Jesus' words from Matthew 28 still ringing in their ears, what did the apostles do to advance Jesus' command?

We don't have to guess at a response to this question! This is where Acts 2 comes in. What can we learn from them, that guides us today as we follow the same trajectory?

Here's the set-up: In Acts 1, we read about Jesus' ascension back into heaven, and the disciples waiting in Jerusalem for the promised Holy Spirit. In Acts 1, the total number of believers is about 120 people, and they're all together in one space (see Acts 1:12–15). Then in Acts 2, the promised Holy Spirit descends in an amazing display—tongues of fire and different languages. This draws a huge crowd, and Peter—one of Jesus' leading apostles—steps out to address this crowd that had gathered. In Acts 2:14–40, Peter talks about Jesus and who He is as God's Messiah, calling the crowd to turn to Jesus.

And then people respond! They repent and turn to Jesus. Acts 2:41 tells us that three thousand people accepted Peter's message about Jesus and were baptized. In a day, the early church grew from 120 to 3,000 followers of Jesus.

The apostles now have a group of 3,000 converts—people who have placed their faith in Jesus as their Lord and Savior. What do they do next? How do they take Jesus' commission in Matthew 28 and apply it? What priorities rise to the top as they make disciples?

What happens next is where we're going to focus. We can't miss this.

> They devoted themselves to the apostles' teaching and to fellowship, to the breaking of bread and to prayer. Everyone was filled with awe at the many wonders and signs performed by the apostles. All the believers were together and had everything in common. They sold property and possessions to give to anyone who had need. Every day they continued to meet together in the temple courts. They broke bread in their homes and ate together with glad and sincere hearts, praising God and enjoying the favor of all the people. And the Lord added to their number daily those who were being saved. (Acts 2:42–47)

There's so much to say about this passage! I'm only going to highlight two things: First, nothing about this passage can be reduced to the individualistic. Notice all the "plural" language. Right away in v. 42: *they* devoted *themselves*; v. 43: *everyone* was filled with awe; v. 44: *all the believers were together*; v. 45: *they* sold property—people voluntarily sacrificing to meet the needs of others in poverty (poverty that likely arose because of persecution and marginalization, when they chose to follow Jesus); v. 46: *they* continued to meet *together* and *they* broke bread in *their* homes and ate *together* . . .

Now you see from God's Word what we've been talking about: Following Jesus is personal, but it is not private. A life of discipleship assumes others, a larger community.

A second thing we need to see from Acts 2 is that a life of discipleship is defined by certain priorities. We see lots of things mentioned in Acts 2:42–47, and there's more than one way to organize what we see emphasized here. But here's one framework that's been practically helpful for the church where I serve and remains faithful to what we see in Acts 2.

This passage gives us three priorities to champion as we make disciples and carry Jesus' Great Commission forward: (1) worship, (2) connect, and (3) serve. Acts 2:42–47 drives these priorities home.[47]

Three Priorities: Worship, Connect, Serve

First, let's see how this passage drips with **worship**: a focus on God and responding to Him. (That's really what worship is: Focusing on a big view of God and responding to who He is.[48]) We see worship in the devotion to God's Word and prayer that we read about. The "breaking of bread" is likely a reference to the Lord's Supper,[49] which churches celebrate in gathered worship, keeping our focus on Jesus and His work. The

101

generosity that we saw is an expression of worship: God has their hearts, not possessions (see also Matt. 6:21, 24; 2 Cor. 8:2–5). We see words like "awe" and "praise" in the passage we read. All of these things are expressions of worship!

Second, **connection** is all over this passage—in words like "fellowship," and "together." The numerical explosion of the church demands a willingness to welcome others and build relationships. We see connection in the gatherings in homes. When you have someone in your home, you connect on a different level!

Third, the idea of **serving** is evident. Serving others is evident in the generosity we've already talked about. For others to open up their homes for meeting spaces, that required a willingness to serve! There's another way serving comes up in this passage that can be easy to overlook: When a group grows in size from 120 to 3,000 in a day, you have to think bigger than yourself. You have to die to some of your preferences and "the way you used to do things." This gospel-growth requires an outreach-oriented, others-centered mindset that is at the heart of service.

Here's a helpful way for me to think about these three priorities: My wife Carrie enjoys gardening. Along with lots of other things she grows, she always grows cucumbers in one of our raised garden beds. Every year before she plants the seeds, she's got a makeshift four-foot-high trellis that she puts over the garden bed. The cucumber plants then climb this trellis as they bear fruit. The reason she does this is because I'm told that cucumbers actually grow better and healthier when they have a trellis to guide their growth. The trellis doesn't make the cucumbers grow. But it facilitates their healthy growth.

Similarly, only God brings growth in our lives (see 1 Cor. 3:6). We are absolutely dependent on Him. At the same time, these priorities help serve as a trellis, facilitating growth in Christlikeness in a healthy way.[50]

So how can we grow into increasing Christlikeness? When we put all this together, we see from Acts 2 that a life of discipleship assumes others, and it's characterized by three priorities: the priority of worship, the priority of connecting with others, and the priority of serving.

Appreciating the Church: Tools for the Toolbox (One Example of How This Can Look)

Now let's talk about what this means in the life of a local church. Here's where I want to get practical and show you some of the ways we're trying to be intentional and practical as a church family at Brookside Church where I serve. We're (imperfectly) championing these same priorities. As a church we're excited about each of these things, and I feel a pastoral responsibility to be able to point us forward in these three areas. So when someone says, "Tim, how can I grow as a follower of Jesus at Brookside?" (or when any Brooksider is asked that same question), we're equipped with an answer that invites them onto a pathway of discipleship.

Before I get into the specifics of things at Brookside, it's important that I quickly mention two disclaimers to keep in mind as you read:

First disclaimer: These words—worship, connect, and serve—express big concepts. It's true that what I'm about to say about worship, connecting, and serving isn't the sum total that could be said about any of these things. My hope is that the way we practice these priorities gives you handles you can grab onto—a trellis that facilitates growth—that invites you further in and encourages you to keep growing.

Second disclaimer: The local church you attend or where you minister may look a little different than the way I describe things here. That's okay. I would even say that's *healthy*. We shouldn't be "copy and paste" identical. I believe there can be various other legitimate, faithful, and good ways these priorities find expression. I hope hearing how one church seeks to embody these priorities prompts your own discussions about how the church where you serve embodies these same biblically rooted priorities, expressed in your particular context.

All right, those are the disclaimers. Let's dig in now to how these priorities find practical expression at the church where I serve.

The first priority I'll talk about is **worship**. Here I have in mind what we call "gathered worship"—what we do when we gather at each of our campuses on Sunday mornings as a church family. We say it this way: "We deliver God-honoring and inspiring services."

At its root, worship is a right view of God and a right response to Him. As we gather, we fill our minds and hearts with a big, right view of God in so many ways. I love how our worship leaders and music team choose songs that fix our eyes on God and help us respond to Him. Our giving that we celebrate as we gather is an expression of worship. We take the Lord's Supper (or communion), remembering Jesus' work on the cross and responding in renewed faith. We celebrate baptisms, which picture the saving work of the gospel in individual lives. We hear from God's Word, filling our minds and fueling our obedience with revealed truth about who God is, what He's done, and how we live faithfully as His followers.

I'm grateful that I grew up in a family that prioritized gathered worship. Even when I didn't want to go to church, my parents let me know I was going. I'm now so glad they did! I first learned how to read the Bible from the way I heard the

Bible preached. I learned the language and posture of worship through songs I was taught to sing. I did some quick math before writing this chapter, and some conservative number crunching indicates that I've been a part of approximately 2,300 gathered Sunday morning worship services in my life so far—and this isn't counting the Wednesday night youth group I attended or Bible college and seminary chapel services. These services have formed me in so many ways!

I was walking through the halls of Brookside not long ago on a Sunday when I saw a dad and his son walk in, with the son wearing his baseball uniform. I thought maybe there was a game after the service, so I said "good luck later on" or something like that, but they corrected me. The son had a game earlier in the morning and they left right when it was over to get here for services. They probably could have come up with a dozen reasons for why they could miss church that Sunday. But they didn't. What an example of prioritizing gathered worship.

Is gathered worship a priority in your life? What commitments do you need to set in place, so that gathered worship is a priority?[51]

Our second priority is **connect**. Simply stated, we grow in community. Others need you, and you need others. We saw community all over the place in the Acts passages, and community stays "all over the place" throughout the entire Bible. In a world that is starving for belonging and healthy relationships, the church should be a place that pursues and models healthy community, community that is defined by God Himself—the One who designed us for community. Our primary expression of connecting is our Groups Ministry, including small groups, medium-sized groups, and classroom environments (we talk about them all the time because they're so important!)—places where you can get to know others and be known by others. Groups have been a staple of my own life—men's group and couples' groups, for example. It's not always convenient. These groups mean early mornings (for my men's group) and some hectic Sunday afternoons (for our couples' group). Convenient? Not always. Worthwhile? Without question.

One short-term group we've offered at Brookside where I serve was a group for empty nesters called "Flourishing in the Third Third of Life." I loved hearing this takeaway from one of the men involved in the group: that this group helped him feel more connected than he had since he started attending. Gathered worship is great! However, we need smaller groups for connection.

Connecting with others is always a little messy. But it forms us in so many ways. Is connecting with other believers a priority in your life?

Our third priority is **serve**. Our gifts are fully expressed by giving back. First Corinthians 12 uses the metaphor of a body when it talks about the church. The apostle Paul talks about how in a healthy body, eyes need hands and hands need eyes and so on. The point he's making there is that we all have something to contribute, and we all need each other. It's a beautiful picture of unity amidst diversity, energized by the Spirit of God. If you're a follower of Jesus, you're a part of the body of Christ. You have something to contribute. And you need what others offer.

Or Ephesians 4 says it this way: "So Christ himself gave the apostles, the prophets, the evangelists, the pastors and teachers, to equip his people for works of service, so that the body of Christ may be built up" (Eph. 4:11–12). There is a direct connection between the body of Christ being built up and the work of serving. Every one of us is needed for this important task. There is opportunity for everyone, factoring in your gifts and capacity. I'm confident there are tangible steps you can take into serving in the next week or two—steps that factor in (1) your passions and gifts, (2) where you've seen God bear fruit through you, and (3) the particular needs of your local church.

For many of you, I'm guessing your church has lots of opportunities that are similar to the church I'm a part of. There's opportunity for small group leaders, people to show up and care for middle schoolers and high schoolers, people to serve the next generation in kids ministry, people who love to work behind the scenes, people to run media ops, serve together at a homeless shelter or crisis women's center, hold doors, reach out to visitors, play guitar, sing, serve those who are struggling in practical ways, and probably dozens of other things!

There are ways to serve on a consistent basis—once a week or once a month—and there are ways to serve more in a one-off sort of way. We call people who serve at Brookside *Difference Makers* because that's exactly what they are—in all the ways people are using their gifts, they're making a difference for the kingdom of God.

Let's be honest: Serving is always a little inconvenient and it comes with a cost. But when you use your gifts you're building up the body of Christ. Plus you're being formed yourself.

Conclusion

"Grandpa, were you a hero in the war?" "No, but I served in the company of heroes." Dick Winters' eyes weren't on himself when he thought about World War II. He knew he was part of something bigger than himself.

In this chapter we've seen that growing as a disciple means we're part of something bigger than just ourselves. Growing as a disciple involves the community of the church. As we worship, connect, and serve—always motivated by God's grace and dependent on Him—we will grow.

I want to finish this chapter with a quote from Colin Hansen and Jonathan Leeman, as they highlight how involvement in the church—an involvement that includes each of the three priorities we've been talking about—forms us in important ways:

> Think of the church as something like waves rolling over rocks. The waves are the church. You and other church members are the rocks. Day after day, year after year, the waves flow without ceasing. They rush over each rock and jostle the rocks against one another. From month to month, you probably won't notice much difference. But over years, even decades, you'll observe the change. As the waves crash and the rocks tumble over one another, their rough edges become smooth. They take on a polished glint in the sun. No two rocks emerge from the process with the same size or shape. But in its own way, each becomes beautiful.[52]

As we grow in Christlikeness, we need each other. Are these priorities (worship, connecting, and serving) that we've seen today from Acts 2 your priorities? What will it look like for you to take a step of faith-filled obedience in response to what you've seen in God's Word?

Questions for Reflection and Discussion

1. Share a time when you were part of a group project or team that accomplished something bigger than what you could have done on your own.

2. Do you think most people think of the community of the church and the practice of discipleship as going hand-in-hand? Why or why not?

3. Three priorities were highlighted in this chapter: (1) worship, (2) connect, (3) serve. Read through Acts 2:42–47 and draw out the connections between what is said in this passage and each of these three priorities.

4. In your own words, summarize each of the three priorities (worship, connect, serve).

5. How do you see these priorities taking shape in the life of the local church you attend? What questions do you have about any of them?

6. What other passages of Scripture or biblical truth come to mind as you think about one or more of these priorities (i.e., worship, connect, and serve)? Read passages of Scripture that come up and share how they relate to any of the three priorities.

7. Why is it important to make sure these three priorities of discipleship are connected to the larger goal of "becoming like Jesus"? Are there ways it can be dangerous to approach these priorities as ends in themselves?

8. How has what you've learned helped you see the value of the local church?

9. Are any of these priorities overlooked in your own personal involvement in the local church? If so, what is one small step you can take?

10. What other questions or comments do you have about anything covered in this chapter that you'd like to discuss?

11. What is your biggest takeaway from what you've discussed so far? Is there a practical step you can take to apply what you've learned?

CHAPTER 7
CULTIVATING WITH CONFIDENCE:
PERSPIRATION AND PERSPECTIVE

My father-in-law, Craig, was a hard worker. A Midwestern farmer his entire life, he got up before the sun and would often still be working out in the cornfields after dark. At his funeral, many of his friends mentioned Craig's strong work ethic, his skill as a farmer, and his personal tenacity. I saw this firsthand over the course of decades. Craig worked hard at creating field conditions that were primed for the corn to grow each season: tilling, fertilizing, bug control, irrigating, leveling, weed control, and I'm sure a whole lot more that I as a "city-slicker" knew nothing about.

But there were also other forces at play alongside Craig's work ethic—other forces entirely outside of my father-in-law's control. Every farmer knows how dependent they are on rain and suitable weather. The miracle of life that is a seed turning into a cornstalk is something a farmer can nurture but never dictate.

Here's the point I'm trying to make: My father-in-law spent his working life cultivating something he could never control. Ultimately other forces at play could determine any season's yield at harvest. But that didn't keep Craig from working tirelessly to cultivate a field that would be conducive to bearing fruit.

In the same way, as followers of Jesus we are cultivating something we can never control. We are called to faithfully pursue godliness in the ways we can and motivated by the grace God gives—"perspiring" with effort toward growing in Christlikeness. We don't accidentally drift into godliness! At the same time, we maintain the perspective that "another force" is at play. However, this "other force" isn't an impersonal force like hail or rain; rather, believers maintain a perspective that this "other force" is the personal, sovereign, and perfectly good triune God who ensures that His saving work will see its way through to completion (Phil. 1:6). Ultimately God brings the growth (see 1 Cor. 3:6–7).

As we pursue the disciplines, we do so with grace-motivated "perspiration" that instills our pursuit with effort and determination. As we pursue the disciplines, we do so with God-fueled "perspective" that anchors our pursuit in dependence and confidence. Consider your own life for a minute: How might a resolute effort ("perspiration") jumpstart your focus and provide forward movement? How might a God-oriented trust ("perspective") motivate your mindset and carry you ahead?

This chapter will now consider more deeply how both *perspiration* and *perspective* play a role in our growth in Christlikeness, ultimately adding up to foster a godly *perseverance* in our Christian faith.

Perspiration

In 2 Peter 1:5, the apostle Peter says to "make every effort" to grow in godly virtues—virtues that can be cultivated through the spiritual disciplines we look at in this book. The NASB translates this phrase "applying all diligence." However you look at it, the idea carries the sense of sweat—exerting ourselves to grow in certain areas.

Peter knows something we need to grasp as well: We'll never drift into godliness. Just like a misaligned car will drift off course, apart from God our hearts are misaligned with a natural drift toward self (Rom. 3:23; Gal. 5:16–17). Our world is misaligned and pulls us away from God (1 John 2:15–17). If we don't "make every effort" to grow in godliness, we'll drift off course.

What gets "make every effort" attention in your life? Is it a goal you're trying to hit at work, so you'll get to the next level in your career? Is it an SAT or ACT score in high school, so you'll have a better chance of getting into the college of your dreams? Is it a relationship—you're striving for someone to notice you, and you're planning your day around catching their attention?

We can all relate to setting stretch goals and then reverse engineering significant aspects of our lives in such a way as to meet those goals. Hitting these goals takes grit and setting aside certain conveniences to achieve our dreams.

So now for the question: Does growing in godliness get "make every effort" attention in your life? Do you keep striving for Christlikeness even when it takes grit, and even when it means setting aside certain conveniences to achieve the greater goal?

To be sure, this grit is motivated by grace—we must not forget that. The apostle Peter knows this. Before his command to "make every effort" in 2 Peter 1:5, Peter has already grounded his readers in God's amazing grace: our faith is found in Christ's righteousness and not our own (2 Peter 1:1); Peter wishes that *grace* and peace may be experienced in abundance through the knowledge of God and of Jesus our Lord (2 Peter 1:2); God's power is what fuels our godliness and we "participate in the divine nature" through His promises and not our works (2 Peter 1:3–4). We must not forget the amazing nature of God's grace.

So yes, God is gracious. More gracious than we can imagine. What good news!

Too often, though, I wonder if we interpret God's grace as leniency—like God doesn't really care one bit how we live because He's gracious. But God's grace doesn't only save us *from* our sin; God's grace also transforms us to live renewed lives. God does care how we live as His followers, and His gracious work provides power and strength for us to see progress in sanctification. (We'll talk about God's gracious work much more soon—in the next section that focuses on "perspective.") We mustn't disconnect grace from growth in a way that would cause the New Testament authors to scratch their heads in confusion and furrow their brow in concern (see Rom. 6:15–18; Eph. 2:8–10; 1 Thess. 4:1–3; Titus 2:11–12).

We see this in 2 Peter 1:5, where Peter starts off the verse with this phrase, "For this very reason . . ." This is a connecting phrase—connecting what Peter is about to say ("make every effort" to grow in godliness, 2 Peter 1:5) with what he had just said about the amazing nature of God's grace. Essentially, Peter is saying "because of God's amazing grace, make every effort to grow in godliness." Grit isn't opposed to grace or disconnected from it. Grit grows out of grace (see 2 Tim. 2:1).[53]

Back to our question: Does growing in godliness get "make every effort" attention in your life? It should—especially if we truly understand the motivating, transformative nature of God's grace.

All the way back in chapter 1, we've already seen how the spiritual disciplines we're looking at in this book can help us train for godliness (1 Tim. 4:7–8). It's no large stretch, then, to make the claim that as we "perspire" in the disciplines (i.e., making every effort to apply them in our lives) we can see growth in godliness.

Perspective

Even as we perspire toward godliness, we can't forget to do so with a proper perspective. This perspective should be fueled by God's grace and shaped by the work of the triune God in securing our salvation and seeing it all the way through to its end in our glorification. Our "make every effort" at godliness is not isolated from God's own great work toward that same end. Indeed, we see every person (Father, Son, and Holy Spirit) in the one Godhead working toward this end.

Our perspective must be shaped by **God the Father's work** for us. We see this very clearly in 1 Thessalonians 4 and 5. In 1 Thessalonians 4:3, the apostle Paul spotlights the importance of sanctification (i.e., growing in godliness) by identifying it very directly with God's will. (Quick side note: Too often we can think God's will is some secret that we need a decoder ring to figure out. Here in 1 Thessalonians 4:3 Paul tells us clearly what God's will is: our growth in godliness. Do you want to know what God's will is for your life? Don't ignore what the Bible says clearly. Start with valuing and pursuing godliness.) And then in what follows—all the way from 1 Thessalonians 4:3 to 1 Thessalonians 5:22—Paul lists a number of commands that should direct the lives of believers. These commands deal with personal and relationship issues, horizontal relationships (human to human) and vertical relationships (humans and God). Every area of our lives is touched as we live in light of these commands.

In other words, as Paul thinks about sanctification there's effort and intentionality we need to show. All of this is simply reinforcing what we've already seen in 2 Peter 1:5: there's a "make every effort" approach to growing in godliness that we can't overlook.

"So how does God the Father work toward this goal?" you may be asking. "Aren't we talking about God's work toward our godliness right now?" We're now ready to answer these questions, with this larger context of 1 Thessalonians 4–5 in mind. Right after this section (1 Thess. 4:3–5:22) that is full to the brim of commands that we apply toward sanctification, 1 Thessalonians moves the spotlight from us to God:

> May God himself, the God of peace, sanctify you through and through. May your whole spirit, soul and body be kept blameless at the coming of our Lord Jesus Christ. The one who calls you is faithful, and he will do it. (1 Thess. 5:23–24)

This "one who calls you" is none other than God the Father Himself.[54] He is faithful to this work of complete sanctification—sanctifying us "through and through" to use the language of the passage. This passage is dripping with a confident God-centeredness: "The one who calls you is faithful, and he will do it" (see also Phil. 1:6; Jude 24–25). Let me say it again so we don't miss it: The work of the Father for us in our sanctification provides confidence to us as His children.

Our perspective needs to be shaped by **God the Son's work.** While much could rightly be said about Christ's work relative to our growth in godliness, the one reality I want to focus on here is *union with Christ.* In his book on this subject,

Rankin Wilbourne explains what *union with Christ* means: "Union with Christ means that you are in Christ and Christ is in you."[55] Thomas Schreiner adds another layer to our understanding: "Union with Christ is the Holy Spirit's work of *joining people to Christ and all his saving benefits*. It is the most comprehensive category of the application of salvation."[56] Christ's righteousness becomes ours (2 Cor. 5:21). Through faith in Jesus, we have "died with Christ" and "will also live with him" (Rom. 6:8). Union with Christ means we are "made alive in Christ," "raised up with Christ," and "seated with him in the heavenly realms" (Eph. 2:5–6).

These realities wrapped up in union with Christ ground our confidence before God not in what we do (which can be so fickle) but in what Christ has done. Wilbourne states:

> It is not the quality or degree of our faith that matters as much as our being united to the object of our faith, the perfect Christ. It is the perfect Christ who saves us, not our imperfect faith or our imperfect obedience. We must be relentless about this. Otherwise, we run the risk of reducing the glory of our salvation in Christ to the smallness of our individual experience of him.[57]

These realities of union with Christ point us toward Christ's continuing work for those who are His and the positive effect of being "in Christ":

> You are more and most yourself when united to Christ. He covers you, he shields you, he represents you before the Father. He also fills you, illumines you, animates you, making you more yourself and more human than you could ever be on your own.[58]

All these realities wrapped up in union with Christ motivate our pursuit of growing in godliness. Earlier I mentioned Romans 6 and Ephesians 2 as passages that ground us in the amazing truths of union with Christ. The apostle Paul—in these same contexts reinforcing the believer's union Christ— also commands dogged pursuit of godliness (see Rom. 6:13, 19; Eph. 2:10; 4:1).

We must not miss the ordering of things here: We are united to Christ through faith in what He has done, and this truth motivates our disciplined pursuit of godliness. We obey *from* approval, not *for* approval. The union we have with Christ because of His work provides confidence to us.

By way of review: As we consider growth in godliness, we must do so with a perspective shaped by the Father's work and the Son's work toward this same end—these truths provide a perspective that injects confidence into our cultivating. To complete our trinitarian survey, we now come to the third person of the Trinity.

Our perspective on godliness and growth must be shaped by **God the Holy Spirit's work**. Again—much deserves to be said on this point; I will limit myself to highlighting one facet of the Spirit's work we don't want to miss.

In various places in the New Testament, the Spirit is called or associated with a "seal" on the life of the believer:

> When you believed, you were marked in him with a seal, the promised Holy Spirit, who is a deposit guaranteeing our inheritance until the redemption of those who are God's possession—to the praise of his glory. (Eph. 1:13b–14)

> And do not grieve the Holy Spirit of God, with whom you were sealed for the day of redemption. (Eph. 4:30)

118

Now it is God who makes both us and you stand firm in Christ. He anointed us, set his seal of ownership on us, and put his Spirit in our hearts as a deposit, guaranteeing what is to come. (2 Cor. 1:21–22)

What does it mean that the Holy Spirit is a "seal"? Ed Clowney summarizes the meaning of this important biblical truth:

By being present in the Spirit, God not only claims us for Himself, He also gives us claim on Him. The Spirit certifies His promise, His pledge to us. Indeed, the Spirit *is* God's keeping of His promise. . . . Paul therefore speaks of the Spirit as God's "down payment" on full and final salvation.[59]

Because followers of Jesus Christ are sealed with the Spirit, our "full and final salvation" is guaranteed—backed with the authority and promise of none other than God Himself. As with the work of the Father and the Son we've seen already, this sealing work of the Holy Spirit provides confidence to us as believers.

Our *perspiration* toward godliness should never be isolated from this trinitarian *perspective* on godliness—the work of the Father, Son, and Spirit pack our perspective with trust, confidence, and hope.

Perseverance

We can now bring the threads together that we've been talking about thus far—perspiration and perspective—and show how these contribute to an important aspect of discipleship: perseverance.

119

Eugene Peterson famously defined discipleship as "a long obedience in the same direction."[60] This "long obedience," however, is not a journey that's easy, frictionless, or unopposed. As we grow in godliness, difficult decisions will need to be made. Obstacles will need to be overcome. Temptations will need to be resisted. Times of plenty and ease can distract us. Longtime habits may need to change. The right way forward won't always be the easy way forward.

John Bunyan underscores this reality of discipleship in his time-tested *The Pilgrim's Progress*, which is rightly a classic.[61] *The Pilgrim's Progress* vividly depicts the Christian life—telling the story of the main character Christian's journey from the City of Destruction to the Celestial City. Christian's journey is fraught with peril, doubt, and things pulling him away from his destination. In both Christian's journey and our own, we need perseverance.

Through all these ups and downs and twists and turns of this "long obedience," then, we need perseverance, a value that the Bible highlights repeatedly. Here's a sampling of verses that drive home this point:

> Because of the increase of wickedness, the love of most will grow cold, but the one who stands firm to the end will be saved. (Matt. 24:12–13)

> Not only so, but we also glory in our sufferings, because we know that suffering produces perseverance; perseverance, character; and character, hope. And hope does not put us to shame, because God's love has been poured out into our hearts through the Holy Spirit, who has been given to us. (Rom. 5:3–5)

Therefore, my dear brothers and sisters, stand firm. Let nothing move you. Always give yourselves fully to the work of the Lord, because you know that your labor in the Lord is not in vain. (1 Cor. 15:58)

Let us not become weary in doing good, for at the proper time we will reap a harvest if we do not give up. (Gal. 6:9)

Therefore, since we are surrounded by such a great cloud of witnesses, let us throw off everything that hinders and the sin that so easily entangles. And let us run with perseverance the race marked out for us, fixing our eyes on Jesus, the pioneer and perfecter of faith. For the joy set before him he endured the cross, scorning its shame, and sat down at the right hand of the throne of God. Consider him who endured such opposition from sinners, so that you will not grow weary and lose heart. (Heb. 12:1–3)

Consider it pure joy, my brothers and sisters, whenever you face trials of many kinds, because you know that the testing of your faith produces perseverance. Let perseverance finish its work so that you may be mature and complete, not lacking anything. (James 1:2–4)

So how can we develop this "muscle" of perseverance? Any answer must factor in the ingredients we've already seen in this chapter—perspiration and perspective. To be abundantly clear on this point, I've pulled all this together into a sort of "perseverance equation":

grace-motivated *perspiration* + Godward-oriented
perspective = biblical *perseverance* toward godliness

Let's briefly walk through the individual pieces of this equation, spelling out how perspiration and perspective each contribute to perseverance.

The ingredient of perspiration is necessary for perseverance, reminding us that perseverance isn't passive. Perseverance takes grit and resolve (perspiration!)—qualities that require something of us. As we've seen, this perspiration includes a commitment to spiritual disciplines that help "train [us] for godliness" (1 Tim. 4:7). To repeat for emphasis, this perspiration must be properly motivated by God's amazing grace. Consider your own life for a minute: How might a fresh commitment to "perspire" in your pursuit of godliness—in all the ways we've talked about in this chapter—help you persevere in the midst of your circumstances right now? What specifically will this perspiring grit look like for you?

Along with perspiration, the ingredient of perspective is necessary for perseverance. In Greek mythology, Sisyphus is a figure who is condemned to an eternal punishment of defeat and futility—tasked with pushing a boulder to the top of a hill, only to have the boulder roll down the hill every time it nears the top. Without biblical perspective, we may wonder at times if our pursuit of godliness through the disciplines is Sisyphean— if our grit is really getting anywhere.

But as we've seen, biblical teaching demonstrates that our pursuit is not hopeless, nor are we "going it alone." God cares deeply about our growth and invests Himself in it. This reality of God's work for His people injects our pursuit with trust, confidence, and hope. Return to considering your own life: How might a fresh perspective—awareness of God's great promises and work on your behalf—help you persevere in the midst of your circumstances?

Conclusion

As a hard-working farmer, my father-in-law spent his working life cultivating something he could never control. But that didn't keep him from farming tirelessly to cultivate a field that would be conducive to bearing fruit. When the season drew to a close, there were always beautiful fields of corn to harvest. What a celebration harvest is for the faithful farmer!

As followers of Jesus, we look forward to the day when our pursuit of godliness (the theological term for this is *sanctification*) becomes the realization of our final state (the theological term for this is *glorification*)—fully renewed into the image Christ (1 John 3:2) and in rich communion with God Himself, in a place where there is no more death, mourning, crying, or pain (Rev. 21:1–5). Until that day when the Lord calls us home in death or when Jesus returns, let's persevere in faith. We perspire toward godliness, motivated by the good news of Jesus' work for us. And we live with perspective, trusting in confidence that God is for us (Rom. 8:28–39; Eph. 1:19).

> May God himself, the God of peace, sanctify you through and through. May your whole spirit, soul and body be kept blameless at the coming of our Lord Jesus Christ. The one who calls you is faithful, and he will do it. (1 Thess. 5:23–24)

Questions for Reflection and Discussion

1. "As followers of Jesus, we are cultivating something we can never control." In your own words, explain what this statement means. Do you agree?

2. Read 2 Peter 1:5. How does this passage emphasize the need for "perspiration" in our pursuit of godliness?

3. What gets "make every effort" attention in your life? Why is growing in godliness worth "make every effort" attention?

4. Review the "Perspective" section in the chapter. What stands out to you most from that section? Why?

5. What does "perspective" add to the pursuit of godliness that simple "perspiration" does not?

6. Review the equation for perseverance: "grace-motivated *perspiration* + Godward-oriented *perspective* = biblical *perseverance* toward godliness." Have any parts of this equation been missing in your pursuit of godliness?

7. Identify one area of life where biblical perseverance is needed. What have you learned in this chapter that can help you persevere faithfully?

8. In this book on spiritual disciplines, why is a chapter on "cultivating with confidence" important to include?

9. What other questions or comments do you have about anything covered in this chapter that you'd like to discuss?

10. What is your biggest takeaway from what you've discussed so far? Is there a practical step you can take to apply what you've learned?

HOW CAN I GROW AS A FOLLOWER OF JESUS?

CHAPTER 8
MATURITY THAT MULTIPLIES: BEING A
DISCIPLE WHO MAKES DISCIPLES

A few years back, my wife, Carrie, our four boys, and I were on a beach in Wilmington, North Carolina, for vacation. It was the first time our boys had seen the ocean, and they loved it. Years later, it remains one of my favorite vacations as a family.

As soon as we got to the ocean, our boys jumped in. The place we got in was about fifty yards away from a long pier that extended out into the ocean. We were bobbing up and down in the waves, having fun in the water, and it wasn't long at all before we looked around and realized we were getting closer and closer to the pier. The lifeguard got our attention—he wanted to make sure we saw there were people fishing off the pier and that we stayed far enough away to avoid their lines. The thing is, we hadn't done any "actual swimming." The drift of the ocean had steadily pulled us away from where we started.

This story is a small example of two very important lessons. Lesson #1: The reality of drift. Even though it didn't feel like we were moving, the ocean was pulling us away from where we started. Lesson #2: The importance of fixed points. We would never have known we were drifting if we didn't have the pier as a reference point.

These lessons go way beyond our one experience in North Carolina. Business leaders know these lessons. In his book *How the Mighty Fall*, Jim Collins identifies stages of decline in a company—companies that once were tremendously influential and then weren't.[62] One of his chapters is titled "The Undisciplined Pursuit of More," and he warns about the decline that can happen when companies get away from the special, unique thing they can be doing and drift into the latest fad or the next growth opportunity—even if it doesn't align with their core purpose and their ability to handle it. Without the fixed point of a clear mission statement—what your company cares about and can be the best at—it's easy to drift as an organization.

You know this personally. Just think about your schedule. If there aren't certain fixed points or priorities in your week, you'll either get talked into lots of things you don't want to do, or you'll have no idea where your time is going. Or think about your budget. It can be so easy to "drift" when swiping a card—just carried along by your next impulse. If there aren't certain priorities that are at the top of your budget, it's easy to swipe here and there, and before you know it, you're at the end of the month with not enough money.

The best way to fight the reality of drift (because it is a fight) is to have fixed points that don't move. Points that we can tether ourselves to in order to keep us from drifting.

Our mission as followers of Jesus must prioritize Jesus' final command to "make disciples" (Matt. 28:19–20). My first book focused on why Jesus is worth following and what it means to follow Him as a disciple—*who* we're becoming, and specific areas of life that need attention as we follow Him. The bulk of this book has focused on *how* we can grow as His followers and "train ourselves for godliness" (1 Tim. 4:7–8).

And now before we're done, we need to consider *where* being a disciple should take us. Or think of it this way: What's my purpose as a follower of Jesus?

There are certainly unique ways each of us will need to answer this question individually. Any answer to this question about *purpose* will need to factor in the unique gifts you have, unique desires and passions that shape what you're about.

At the same time, any answer to this question—"What's my purpose as a follower of Jesus?"—will need to factor in a purpose our Lord gives that applies to every disciple. Here it is in a sentence, just to get it in front us: **As followers of Jesus, we are called to be disciples who make disciples.** Other people are Jesus followers and growing closer to Jesus because of our influence.

Clarity on this purpose that Jesus gives is so important. It's easy to drift! If you're a follower of Jesus, you should want to care about the things Jesus cares about. It's galvanizing to know you are aligned with the mission of what God Himself is doing in and for the world—there's nothing more important!

Or if you've gotten this far into the book and you're on the very front end of starting to investigate Jesus, His claims, and what it means to follow Him, I'm glad you're still with me! Pay attention in this chapter, and you'll learn a little more about why followers of Jesus talk about Jesus the way we do. Even more than that, I hope you'll be intrigued about the purpose that following Jesus offers, and how that can instill purpose in your own life about the things that matter most. Following Jesus gives you direction and purpose.

In this chapter I want to look at four "fixed points" we need to keep in mind regarding the purpose Jesus gives His followers.

We'll drill down into (1) the focus of our mission, (2) the scope of our mission, (3) the means of our mission, and (4) the stakes of our mission.

The Focus of Our Mission

Jesus Himself provides focus to our mission in Matthew 28:18–20. (I hope this passage is familiar by now!) "Then Jesus came to them and said, 'All authority in heaven and on earth has been given to me'" (Matt. 28:18). The gospel of Matthew makes it abundantly clear that Jesus' authority is a good authority—one that serves, sacrifices, and saves. In what He says next, Jesus gives us this mission that applies to every one of His followers:

> Therefore go and make disciples of all nations, baptizing them in the name of the Father and of the Son and of the Holy Spirit, and teaching them to obey everything I have commanded you. And surely I am with you always, to the very end of the age."
> (Matt. 28:19–20)

The single, driving imperative in that passage is this: Make disciples. Everything else that maybe sounds like a command is actually modifying the command—telling us how we make disciples. (We make disciples by "going," "baptizing," and "teaching" for obedience. Each of these words is a participle in the Greek.)

The focal point of what Jesus is saying is this: "Make disciples." This command is our first fixed point.

This statement in Matthew 28 is what drives our mission as God's people. It isn't just something for paid church staff to do, nor is it intended only for the "really involved people" who

130

serve. This command is for every follower of Jesus. We should all feel ownership in this.

Disciples make disciples.

This mission—making disciples—needs to be a fixed point for us. I've heard it said that pilots are taught what's called a "one in sixty rule"—after sixty miles, a one degree error in heading will result in straying off course by one mile.[63] So what that means is this: If you're flying from Omaha (where I live) to Dallas—a distance of a little more than six hundred miles—and if you take off from Omaha just one degree off, you'll miss the runway in Dallas by ten miles. If you're off by thirty degrees, you'd better land in Austin. You'd miss the city of Dallas entirely.

Little degrees of drift can pull us off course in big ways.

There can be so many distractions pulling you off course from this mission Jesus gives us—even just by a few degrees. The ever-changing news cycle that's vying for your attention. Another fad to chase. The constant distraction of social media always within arm's reach. A relationship in your life that's pulling you away from Jesus. The frenetic pace of our lives where there's always another email to reply to, another task you can accomplish, another thing that needs to be done.

To be sure: It's good to stay aware of current events. Relationships are good. It's not bad to have goals, keep an intentional schedule, and accomplish tasks. But any of these things can become distractions when they take our eyes off the mission Jesus gives us: We are to be disciples who make disciples.

The Scope of Our Mission

We find our second fixed point, the scope of our mission, spelled out in Acts 1:8. Jesus is talking to His apostles right before He ascends back into heaven, and check out what He says. "But you will receive power when the Holy Spirit comes on you; and you will be my witnesses *in Jerusalem, and in all Judea and Samaria, and to the ends of the earth*" (Acts 1:8).

Jesus is basically telling the apostles to think in terms of concentric circles here; these circles carry implications that remain instructive for us still today. Jerusalem was home base for them. It was familiar. It's where they already knew people and how things are done. Jesus wants them to be His witnesses—to talk about Jesus with others—right where they're at. Living on mission for Jesus isn't just something people do overseas in different cultures. Living on mission starts with the relationships around you right now—in your family or neighborhood or college campus or workplace.

The next circle out from Jerusalem in Acts 1:8 is "Judea and Samaria." For the average Jewish person in the first century, the region of Samaria was a place to avoid, even though it was in very close proximity to them. Samaritans were looked down upon and there were centuries of issues making the relationship between these two people groups complicated and difficult. But Jesus still includes Samaria in the scope of His mission. Why? Because all people matter to God.

Which people in proximity to you are hard for you to love? Someone that's awkward to be around or that makes you uncomfortable or that's just different from you? Is there someone around your life that you do your best to avoid? What can you do to help this person feel seen? Loved? Start praying for the opportunity to talk about Jesus with them.

The final circle in Acts 1:8 is "the ends of the earth." There are so many ways to participate in God's mission around the globe through praying, giving, and going. Not long before I wrote this chapter, twelve college students who attend the church where I serve got back from a week in the Dominican

Republic, supporting one of our strategic partnerships there—a ministry that does so much with church planting in unreached areas of that country. I love the vision this trip gave those students of what Jesus is doing to build His church. I talked with one of the students after the trip and he said it was maybe "the best week of his life." He listed a number of reasons for this, including this one: "I was able to learn from another culture while also talking about my faith with others and how they came to faith." Talk about a mission mindset!

I'll say it again: There are so many ways to participate in God's mission around the globe through praying, giving, and going—either short-term or long-term. Some of you reading this may end up overseas long-term through a missions agency. God is still calling people to serve Him this way!

We know what our mission is: Make disciples. And we know it's a big mission, starting where we're at and extending out. We witness to Jesus within our families, across the street, throughout the city, and around the globe.

Now how can we advance this mission? Answering this question brings us to the next fixed point we need to keep in view.

The Means of Our Mission

We've already seen the answer in Acts 1:8. In the previous section we focused on the end of this verse; now let's look closely at the beginning of the verse: "*But you will receive power when the Holy Spirit comes on you; and you will be my witnesses* in Jerusalem, and in all Judea and Samaria, and to the ends of the earth."

How can we advance the mission Jesus gives us? Only by the power of the Holy Spirit and by each of us getting involved.

One of the great truths of Christianity is that followers of Jesus have the Holy Spirit dwelling in us. The Holy Spirit is the third person of the Trinity, and He energizes and empowers our mission. His presence in our lives is so important that at the very end of Luke, Jesus tells His apostles to wait in Jerusalem until the Spirit comes. We don't want to even try to do ministry without Him!

Becky Pippert drives home the vital importance of the Holy Spirit in her book *Stay Salt*:

> Our lack of dependence on the Spirit's power is perhaps the single most glaring deficiency in the modern Western church. . . . The early church demonstrated great courage in their witness and were bursting at the seams with spiritual power, even while they were experiencing catastrophic consequences for proclaiming the gospel. We, on the other hand, often shrink back at merely a raised eyebrow. . . . To live as Christ's witnesses in the 21st century, it is critical that we embrace the power of the Spirit, who resides in us."[64]

How can we advance the mission Jesus gives? We need the Holy Spirit. We bathe everything we're doing in prayer. We learn to discern and follow His prompting. And we step out in faith as He leads and works around us and ahead of us.

We need the Holy Spirit.

And we each need to get involved. "Being Christ's witness" that Acts 1:8 talks about is for every follower of Jesus.

Let's go a little further into the book of Acts to see how this mission plays out: In Acts 7–8 a significant wave of persecution hits the early church. An early church leader named Stephen is stoned to death, and that sparks even more persecution.

> On that day a great persecution broke out against the church in Jerusalem, and all except the apostles were scattered throughout Judea and Samaria.

[They're getting into the next concentric circle!]
Godly men buried Stephen and mourned deeply for
him. But Saul began to destroy the church. Going
from house to house, he dragged off both men and
women and put them in prison. (Acts 8:1b–3)

I can't imagine how difficult this must've been! Fear.
Displacement. Grief.

Yet they persist with mission.

We see this in the very next verse. Acts 8:4: "Those who had
been scattered preached the word wherever they went."

That "preaching the word" doesn't mean they were
delivering thirty-five-minute messages like some people maybe
think about preaching today. It's shorthand for talking about
Jesus. They were so in love with Jesus that they couldn't *not* talk
about Him.[65] This is sharing the gospel—the good news about
Jesus. It's talking about Jesus in the context of our lives. This
priority is for every follower of Jesus.

Let me give you one way to approach this topic that's been
helpful for me in my relationships—see the diagram below and
the brief explanation that follows.

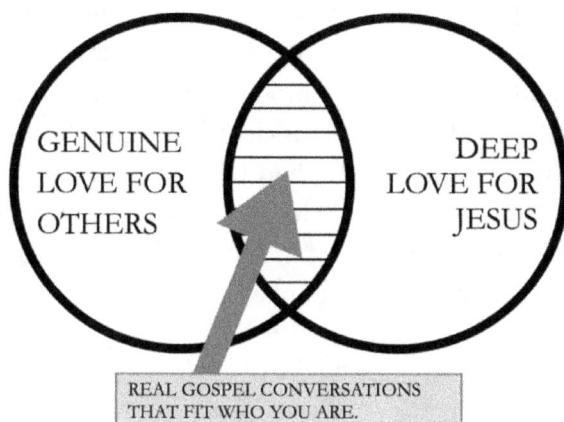

Figure 1. Cultivating gospel conversations

We want to love people so well that our genuine compassion for them is evident. People are not projects. And we want to love Jesus so deeply that we can't not talk about Him. Where those two things come together (genuine love for others and deep love for Jesus) is the "sweet spot" where gospel conversations happen in a way that fits who you are.

I was listening to a podcast not long ago, and the guy being interviewed was talking about evangelism, and he simply asked, "Who do you grieve over?"[66] What relationship do you care so deeply about that imagining eternity without that person does something in your heart? There's clear compassion here. This is about relationships. And there's intentionality. We're talking about Jesus.

As you talk about Jesus in genuine relationship with others, eventually you'll be able to share your own story—who you were before following Jesus, why you chose to follow Him, and the difference He's making in your life. You'll hear about their problems, and you can ask, "How can I pray for you?" You'll have opportunity to invite them to join you at a church service and then talk about it.

You can walk through a gospel presentation, clearly sharing about who Jesus is and why we need Him. This is where tools are valuable.[67] Personally, I'm a fan of twowaystolive.com—a user-friendly website that is mobile-friendly and walks people through the good news of Jesus clearly and simply.

Acts 8:4 says "those who had been scattered preached the word wherever they went." How can you take the gospel to the places you are? Every one of us is needed for the mission Jesus calls us to. You have a role to play.

The Stakes of Our Mission

I'm only going to very briefly touch on the fourth fixed point of our mission: The stakes of our mission.

In John 10:10, Jesus is describing His mission, and He says, "The thief comes only to steal and kill and destroy; I have come that they may have life, and have it to the full."

The "full life" Jesus is talking about here isn't only life in relationship with Him now. Jesus is also thinking about eternal life. Life with Him that starts when we believe (our experience of it is partial yet true, see Phil. 3:7–11). And this life carries forward beyond death into eternity, where we'll experience it fully (see Phil. 3:12–14, 20–21).

The stakes of our mission are eternal stakes.

As Jesus' disciples, we experience life the way God our Creator designed it. We experience relationship with Jesus, and we find our deepest satisfaction in Him. Those who place their faith in Jesus are promised eternal life and a future in God's restored creation where everything is finally and fully the way it's supposed to be.

Those who resist God and refuse to bow the knee to Jesus in this life will not experience this promised eternal life. A hard truth the Bible teaches is that those who refuse Jesus, those who don't know Him, will spend eternity separated from Him in hell—a place of torment, regret, and isolation (see Dan. 12:2; Matt. 7:21–23; 25:41–46; 2 Thess. 1:8–9; Rev. 20:15).

We can't forget the stakes of our mission.

Conclusion

It's so easy to drift. And you won't always know you're drifting! You need fixed points around you. As we finish up this book on how we grow as followers of Jesus, we see that following Jesus includes an others-facing posture. It's about thinking bigger than just yourself. Following Jesus isn't just about *being* a disciple. It's also about *making* disciples. As followers of Jesus, we are called to be disciples who make disciples. It's about multiplication.

We need fixed points to keep us from drifting. We need to remember *the focus of our mission*: Make disciples. Introduce people to Jesus and help them follow Him. How does the clarity of this mission shape your priorities this week?

We need to remember *the scope of our mission*: Within our homes, across the street, throughout the city, and around the globe. What intentional step toward others do you need to take? How can you help someone else see the beauty of who Jesus is and what He's done—maybe for the very first time? How can you help someone else grow as a follower of Jesus? Even as you read this, is there someone that comes to mind right now?

We need to remember *the means of our mission*. We need the Holy Spirit. Each one of us has a role to play. How can you more actively depend on the Holy Spirit this week? What genuine relationship do you have with someone who doesn't know Jesus, where you can bring Him into that? Or if no one comes to mind—if you don't have a relationship with someone who doesn't know Jesus—how can you start to cultivate a relationship like that? Pray about this and ask God to bring someone to mind.

We need to remember *the stakes of our mission*. How does the reality of heaven and hell spark compassion and motivate mission?

Let's all keep Matthew 28:18–20 in front of us:

> Then Jesus came to them and said, "All authority in heaven and on earth has been given to me. Therefore go and make disciples of all nations,

baptizing them in the name of the Father and of the Son and of the Holy Spirit, and teaching them to obey everything I have commanded you. And surely I am with you always, to the very end of the age.

Questions for Reflection and Discussion

1. Read Matthew 28:18–20 and Acts 1:8. In your own words, summarize what these passages say about the mission of followers of Jesus.

2. What can distract you from being a part of this mission personally?

3. In Acts 1:8, we see that telling others about Jesus starts where we are (our "Jerusalem"). What can you do to live on mission in your current context (home, school, work, neighborhood, etc.)? What questions or concerns do you have about this?

4. In Acts 1:8, the mission Jesus gives extends to "Samaria." Samaria was in proximity to Jerusalem but was often avoided by Jews. Who are you in proximity to that you tend to avoid—because they make you uncomfortable or are simply different from you? What can you do to help this person feel seen and loved?

5. In Acts 1:8, we also see that the mission of Jesus should reach "the ends of the earth." How can you grow in your awareness of what God is doing around the world?

6. Gospel conversations (that is, telling others about Jesus) flourish at the intersection of genuine care for others and deep love for Jesus. With this in mind, answer the following questions:

- Practically speaking, how can you build genuine friendships with people who don't know Jesus? Share from experience if you can.

- Make a list of ways you can bring Jesus into these conversations and help point others to Jesus in either informal or more formal ways.

- When you think about talking about Jesus with someone who doesn't know Jesus, what feelings, thoughts, or questions come to your mind? Explain.

7. Why is the work the Holy Spirit so important when talking to others about Jesus? What does it look like to depend on the Spirit in these conversations and stay attuned to His leading?

8. Reflect back on key relationships that helped you (and/or are still helping you) grow as a disciple. What are the characteristics of this relationship that were especially influential in your own formation? How does knowing what helped you grow help you disciple others?

9. What other questions or comments do you have about anything covered in this chapter that you'd like to discuss?

10. What is your biggest takeaway from what you've discussed so far? Is there a practical step you can take to apply what you've learned?

CONCLUSION

"Train yourself to be godly" (1 Tim. 4:7). All the way back in chapter 1, we set our sights on this goal: godliness (or Christlikeness). As we follow Jesus, we should grow in godliness. This growth may not happen as fast as you want, there will be twists and turns along the way, and some of the ways growth takes shape may not be what you'd expect. But over the course of time, we should be able to point to genuine ways we're growing in godliness. Godliness is worth it! Don't forget the value of godliness that the apostle Paul underscores: This godliness holds promise "for both the present life and the life to come" (1 Tim. 4:8).

In chapter 1 we reviewed what this picture of godliness encompasses—six areas of life, or "6 Cs," that will be affected as we grow in godliness. To keep these areas of life fresh in mind, they've been accessible in appendix 1, and I'll briefly highlight them again here:

- **Commitment:** Following Jesus changes my allegiance.

- **Communion with God:** Following Jesus opens up intimacy with God through knowing Christ in the most satisfying and enriching of relationships.

- **Community with others:** Following Jesus means belonging and transformed relationships.

- **Character:** Following Jesus will change me from the inside out.

- **Conduct:** Following Jesus transforms the way I live and what I actually do.

- **Commission:** Following Jesus gives me purpose and sends me out on mission.

If that's a picture of *who* we're becoming, the majority of this book has focused on *how* we grow—presenting biblical, actionable practices that cultivate growth. We've spent time on the disciplines of Bible engagement, prayer, fasting, solitude, and local church involvement. We've anchored our trust in God for this growth (the chapter on "Cultivating with Confidence") and established the necessary missional mindset that should accompany all of this ("the chapter on "Maturity That Multiplies").

Now, in this concluding chapter, I simply want to help you start to draw out ways you can connect the practices with the picture—that is, how can the practices discussed in this book cultivate the picture of godliness we're pursuing? Remember, these practices are not ends in themselves. We're training ourselves *for godliness*. How can the spiritual disciplines help us grow?

Think of the next few pages as a workbook exercise you can do individually or with a group. The layout is straightforward: You'll find each chapter title in this book listed below. Below each chapter, each of the six "Cs" of the picture of discipleship are included.

Here's where your participation comes in: For each chapter (i.e., for each spiritual discipline), I want you to think through this question: **"How can this spiritual discipline help me grow in one or more of these '6Cs'?"** You're reflecting on how Bible engagement, for example, can help your growth in communion with God or conduct. Or another example: You're reflecting on how solitude can shape your character or commitment.

Here are four things to keep in mind before you proceed: First, don't feel any pressure to fill out all six Cs for each individual spiritual practice. That may feel forced or be too overwhelming. Second, refer back to any chapters from the book as needed. Third, most people will complete what's below in a series of sittings. Do this exercise at a pace that works for you. Fourth and finally, this exercise won't be exhaustive or the "final word" on what could be included. My intention is that this exercise *begins* or *furthers* the process of thinking how spiritual practices cultivate Christlikeness.

The value in this exercise is that it will help cement what you've learned in this book and connect it to your ongoing growth. Here's the question to ask yourself for each chapter listed below:

"How can this spiritual discipline help me grow in one or more of these '6Cs'?"

BIBLE ENGAGEMENT: DELIGHT AND DILIGENCE

"How can this spiritual discipline help me grow in one or more of these '6Cs'?"

- Commitment:

- Communion with God:

- Community with others:

- Character:

- Conduct:

- Commission:

PRAYER: PRIORITY AND PRIVILEGE

"How can this spiritual discipline help me grow in one or more of these '6Cs'?"

- Commitment:

- Communion with God:

- Community with others:

- Character:

- Conduct:

- Commission:

FASTING: EXPRESSING AN APPETITE FOR GOD

"How can this spiritual discipline help me grow in one or more of these '6Cs'?"

- Commitment:

- Communion with God:

- Community with others:

- Character:

- Conduct:

- Commission:

SOLITUDE: CROWDING OUR LIVES WITH GOD

"How can this spiritual discipline help me grow in one or more of these '6Cs'?"

- Commitment:

- Communion with God:

- Community with others:

- Character:

- Conduct:

- Commission:

APPRECIATING THE CHURCH: THE ROLE OF THE CHURCH IN SPIRITUAL FORMATION

"How can this spiritual discipline help me grow in one or more of these '6Cs'?"

* Commitment:

* Communion with God:

* Community with others:

* Character:

* Conduct:

* Commission:

CULTIVATING WITH CONFIDENCE: PERSPIRATION AND PERSPECTIVE

"How can this perspective help me grow in one or more of these '6Cs'?"

- Commitment:

- Communion with God:

- Community with others:

- Character:

- Conduct:

- Commission:

MATURITY THAT MULTIPLIES: BEING A DISCIPLE WHO MAKES DISCIPLES

"How can this perspective help me grow in one or more of these '6Cs'?"

- Commitment:

- Communion with God:

- Community with others:

- Character:

- Conduct:

- Commission:

Conclusion

Finally, thank you for reading this book and processing it in the ways you have. The older I get, the more I want to keep growing as a disciple personally—there's no ceiling to this pursuit! The longer I'm in ministry, the more I want others to experience the "promise for the present life and also for the life to come" (1 Tim. 4:8) that training in godliness brings. Writing this book has restirred my own heart for the richness and rightness of following Jesus, and I hope reading it has served you as well. Thanks again.

APPENDIX 1

AN ORIENTATION TO 6C DISCIPLESHIP

In a previous book, *What Does It Mean to Follow Jesus?*, I provide a **picture** of discipleship—a holistic picture of discipleship that is informed by Jesus' teaching and consistent with a New Testament view of Christlikeness. My goal is that this previous book gives clear direction to our discipleship, identifying six areas we can be increasingly growing in as followers of Jesus (what I call the "6C picture of discipleship").

While I hope you'll dig more deeply into *What Does It Mean to Follow Jesus?* in its entirety, below I've provided a brief orientation to the 6Cs it more fully develops. By including this appendix here, my goal is to help anchor the practices of discipleship in this book with the picture of discipleship in the previous work—keeping our effort in "training for godliness" (the focus of this current book) on the right track and moving in the right direction. The spiritual disciplines must not become ends in themselves, but rather are best approached as God-given, grace-dependent means by which we grow in conformity to Christ.

In this appendix, for each of the 6Cs I identify the "C" and I provide the core statement of that "C," which I included in *What Does It Mean to Follow Jesus?* I then expand beyond that with fresh material, providing a paragraph that summarizes the "C" in a way that's consistent with what's presented in my first book, along with key verses related to the "C."

C – Commitment

- **Core statement:** Following Jesus changes my allegiance.

- **Summary and key verses:** Following Jesus changes my allegiance. There is a decisive commitment to follow Him (Rom. 10:9–10; Col. 1:13–14) and a daily decision to live in light of this commitment (Luke 9:23; Rom. 12:1). This commitment is motivated by God's grace (Eph. 2:8–10) and includes orienting our lives around Christ and a willingness to be formed by Him (Col. 1:28–29).

C – Communion with God

- **Core statement:** Following Jesus opens up intimacy with God through the Spirit.

- **Summary and key verses:** We are designed for experiential relationship with God (Gen. 3:8; Ps. 16:11; Matt. 1:23; John 15:15; Eph. 1:17; Rev. 21:3–4). This relationship is the most satisfying and enriching of all relationships (Ps. 84:10; Phil. 3:7–11). We can know God and be reconciled to Him (Rom. 5:1). We are known by God as His adopted sons and daughters through the Holy Spirit (Gal. 4:6–7) in a relationship where we are secure, known, and valued.

C – Community with Others

- **Core statement:** Following Jesus means belonging and transformed relationships.

- **Summary and key verses:** As followers of Jesus, we belong to the family of God that is defined by faith— not blood or physical descent (John 1:12; Mark 3:31– 35; Eph. 2:11–22). This community is marked by their devotion to God and their love for one another (Matt. 22:36–40; John 13:34–35; Acts 2:42–47; Rom. 12:9– 21; New Testament "one anothers"[68]). Gathering together in community is a priority that should not be compromised (Heb. 10:24–25; 1 Peter 2:4–5).

C – Character

- **Core statement:** Following Jesus will change me from the inside out.

- **Summary and key verses:** The more someone gets to know disciples of Jesus, the more they should see attractive and compelling virtue—namely, the fruit the Spirit bears in us (Gal. 5:22–23; see also James 3:13– 18; 2 Peter 1:5–7). Followers of Jesus must care deeply about who they are on the inside (i.e., their "heart," Prov. 4:23), which begins with the new heart Jesus provides through His grace (2 Cor. 5:17; see also Jer. 31:33; Ezek. 36:26–27; Matt. 5:17–48)—a new heart that transforms our direction and desires (Eph. 4:22– 24). It must be remembered that cultivating hearts in which this fruit grows requires both patience and persistence.

C – Conduct

- **Core statement:** Following Jesus transforms the way I live and what I actually do.

- **Summary and key verses:** Following Jesus is personal but it is not private—God's transforming grace should take shape in our lives visibly (Matt. 5:13–16; 7:24–27; Phil. 1:27; 1 Tim. 4:12; Titus 3:11–12). This conduct isn't a way to earn God's favor, but is rather evidence of His gracious work in you and of a life that is being renewed by Him (Eph. 2:8–10). Christian conduct must be defined by such phrases as gospel-motivated, Godward-oriented, patient, persevering, and progressive (not perfectionistic).

C – Commission

- **Core statement:** Following Jesus gives me purpose and sends me out on mission.

- **Summary and key verses:** Our commission isn't just to be disciples; our commission includes the command to make disciples (Matt. 28:19–20). "Multiplication" and "living sent" must be part of our mindset (see Acts 8:4; 11:19–20; 13:1–3). This command to make disciples includes both sharing Jesus (evangelism) and showing Jesus (visibly good deeds, or "public good") in faithful, dependent, courageous, and winsome ways (Matt. 5:16; Luke 10:25–37; Acts 1:8; Col. 4:2–6; 1 Peter 2:11–12).

APPENDIX 2
OBSTACLES TO GROWTH: SIN (AND HOW TO DEAL WITH IT)

The reality of sin—along with the importance of fighting sin and responding to it—cannot be ignored in a book on spiritual growth. In what follows you'll find a brief orientation to understanding and responding to sin, as a follower of Jesus.

The movie version of J. R. R. Tolkien's *Fellowship of the Ring*[69] contains a powerful, attention-grabbing scene when the wizard Gandalf and his fellowship of traveling companions are fleeing the mines of Moria on their quest to destroy the ring of power. Just before they reach the exit, they must cross the bridge of Khazad-dûm.

Before everyone can safely cross the bridge and exit, however, they're confronted by the Balrog—an evil monster from the shadow world determined to stop them. Heroically, Gandalf battles the Balrog (can anywhere else hear him commanding, "You shall not pass!" right now?). Gandalf thrusts his staff into the bridge and the bridge on which the Balrog stands crumbles, sending him hurling into the pit below. The Balrog has been defeated! As movie watchers, we breathe a sigh of relief.

But the fight isn't done yet. As he falls, the Balrog uses his whip to catch Gandalf's ankle and pull him down with him into the pit. Though the Balrog is ultimately defeated, he is determined to bring Gandalf down with him.

This illustration tells us something about sin.

A thorough understanding of formation into Christlikeness cannot neglect the reality of sin—understanding the basics of its nature and how to deal with it as followers of Jesus. While believers have been rescued from the ultimate penalty for sin (John 5:24; Rom. 6:23) and its reigning power in our lives (Rom. 6:17–18), the presence and pull of sin remains (Gal. 5:17; 1 John 1:8; see also Heb. 11:25).

Here is the connecting point with the *Fellowship of the Ring* illustration: Though sin and Satan have been defeated through the work of Christ (Rom. 5:6; 8:1–2; Col. 2:13–15), sin is determined to take us down with it (Rom. 6:13–14).

We need to take sin seriously.

Cornelius Plantinga draws out why we need to take sin seriously in his book *Not the Way It's Supposed to Be: A Breviary of Sin*:

> In this book I am trying to retrieve an old awareness that has slipped and changed in recent decades. The awareness of sin used to be our shadow. Christians hated sin, feared it, fled from it, grieved over it. . . . But the shadow has dimmed. Nowadays, the accusation *you have sinned* is often said with a grin, and with a tone that signals an inside joke. At one time, this accusation still had the power to jolt

people. . . . As a child growing up in the [1950s and
attending church], I think I heard as many sermons
about sin as I did about grace.[70]

Why does this "dimming" and "change" in awareness of sin
matter? Plantinga tells us. I'll repeat the last sentence of his
quote you just read, that will help carry us forward in
Plantinga's train of thought:

As a child growing up in the [1950s and attending
church], I think I heard as many sermons about sin
as I did about grace. The assumption in those days
seemed to be that you couldn't understand either
without understanding both. . . . My goal, then, is
to renew the knowledge of a persistent reality that
used to invoke in us fear, hatred, and grief. Many of
us have lost this knowledge, and we ought to regret
the loss. For slippage in our consciousness of sin, like
most fashionable follies, may be pleasant, but it is
also devastating. Self-deception about our sin is a
narcotic,   a   tranquilizing   and   disorienting
suppression of our central nervous system.[71]

Plantinga then shows us what we've lost in this "slippage"
and "self-deception" about sin:

Moral beauty begins to bore us. The idea that the
human race needs a Savior sounds quaint.[72]

In other words, if sin isn't serious, you'll struggle to see the
sweetness of Christlikeness. The idea that you need a Savior
will seem abstract, and the work of Christ for you will bring a
bland, "meh" response. The life-transforming, godliness-
fueling power of the gospel will seem either irrelevant or

unattractive. There will be diminished drive to "train yourself for godliness" (1 Tim. 4:7–8) if sin isn't dreadful.

In this appendix, then, I want to provide an introductory framework for understanding and addressing sin in a way that facilitates what we're trying to do in this book—growing in Christlikeness and cultivating Christian formation. We will focus first on what we learn about the seriousness of sin from Genesis 3—where sin enters creation. We will see that sin is serious because of what it is (i.e., the nature of sin) and because of what it does (i.e., the effect or consequences of sin).

Genesis 3 also equips us to know how to respond to sin and temptation. We see wrong ways of responding in the example of Adam and Eve. By learning from their *wrong response*, we discover some practical takeaways regarding what a *right response* involves.

Genesis 3 goes beyond simply the "bad example" of Adam and Eve's fall into sin, however. We also see how God responds to sin. In God's response to sin, Genesis 3 points us forward to the ultimate defeat of sin. This ultimate defeat of sin in the work of Christ energizes and empowers us with the ability to respond to sin the right way.

Taking Sin Seriously: The Nature of Sin

To take sin seriously, we first need to understand its nature. When we see the nature of something—what it *is*—we're best able to evaluate it and know how to respond to it. Let's walk through Genesis 3:1–7 and see what it says about the nature of sin.

> Now the serpent was more crafty than any of the wild animals the Lord God had made. He said to the woman, "Did God really say, 'You must not eat from any tree in the garden'?" (Gen. 3:1)

Here Genesis introduces us to a new character in the story—the serpent, someone we've not yet met. Genesis 3 doesn't spend any time answering questions we often wonder about, questions like, "Where did the serpent come from?" or "How can he talk?" for example. What Genesis 3 does tell us is that he's another creature—he's not on par with God in any sort of dualistic sense. There is only one God and even this serpent is under His authority as a created being.

Indeed, at the very end of our Bibles, Revelation 12:9 tells us that the devil, or Satan, is that "ancient serpent." So we know that Satan is either embodying this snake or is at least behind the snake's activity. But Eve doesn't know this. All she knows is she's asked a question.

Genesis 3 includes the serpent's speech—a question that clearly undermines God's authority. "Did God really say . . . ?" Don't miss what we can learn about Satan's tactics here. He doesn't come in with a full-frontal assault, but subtly. With a question. Deceitfully. Sin's approach is often more covert than overt.

So how does Eve respond?

> The woman said to the serpent, "We may eat fruit from the trees in the garden, but God did say, 'You must not eat fruit from the tree that is in the middle of the garden, and you must not touch it, or you will die.'" (Gen. 3:2–3)

We need to slow down for a minute so we don't miss a key point in what's going on here. Eve is referring to God's original command to Adam that came a chapter earlier in Genesis 2:16–17, where we read "And the LORD God commanded the man, 'You are free to eat from any tree in the garden; but you must not eat from the tree of the knowledge of good and evil, for when you eat from it you will certainly die.'"

When commentators compare God's original command in chapter 2 with Eve's response in chapter 3, they notice shades of difference—enough difference that it's noticeable. And important. If we were to line up what God says in Genesis 2 with how Eve responds to the serpent in Genesis 3, we'd see that she both *softens* God's command and *adds* a little to it.[73] This misrepresentation of God's Word catches our attention as readers of Genesis. We begin to get concerned for how the situation will continue to unfold. Warning signs are flashing. It's so important to know God's Word well as we respond to temptation (see Ps. 119:9–11 and the way Jesus responds to Satan's temptations with God's Word in Matthew 4:1–11)!

Let's return to Genesis 3: "You will not certainly die," the serpent said to the woman (Gen. 3:4). Now the serpent is directly contradicting God's Word! "For God knows that when you eat from it your eyes will be opened, and you will be like God, knowing good and evil" (Gen. 3:5). So much more could be said here: Satan's claims should have gotten Eve's attention. She was already "like God"—created in His image (Gen. 1:26–27)! She already knew good (after all, she's in the midst of God's "very good" creation—see Gen. 1:31); why would she want to learn evil?! Temptation too often blurs and confuses our ability to think clearly—taking what is so often good and twisting it, corrupting it, for evil ends.

The bottom line is that Satan is appealing to Eve's individualism here—her autonomy. Rather than seeing herself as living for God, under His amazingly good authority, and rather than finding her identity the way God designed it and within His purpose, Satan says Eve can be like God.[74]

This is the root of sin, when you peel everything else back. God is removed from His rightful place and His good authority in our lives, and something else takes His place. We go our own way instead of His. One of my professors at seminary, D. A. Carson, called this the "de-godding of God."[75]

As we watch this dialogue, our eyes go back to Eve. Once again—how does Eve respond?

> When the woman saw that the fruit of the tree was good for food and pleasing to the eye, and also desirable for gaining wisdom, she took some and ate it. She also gave some to her husband, who was with her, and he ate it. (Gen. 3:6)

It blows my mind that Adam was right there with her the whole time, and he did nothing! Why didn't he step in or speak up?! He's passive! This would be a whole other chapter so I won't say much, but at least let me talk to the men who are reading this right now: Let's not be passive! Let's stand up for the things of God!

> Then the eyes of both of them were opened, and they realized they were naked; so they sewed fig leaves together and made coverings for themselves. (Gen. 3:7)

From here forward, sin has entered the world. In theological language, this is called "the Fall" of humanity—the Fall from goodness into sin.

Remember the question we're asking: What is it about the nature of sin that should make us take it seriously? We should take sin seriously because it's cosmic treason. We are removing the good and perfect God from His place of authority and putting something else in His place. It's not an exaggeration to say that sin subverts and distorts reality. This isn't small, and it isn't cute. It's a rebellion against God's design for our lives, and His identity as our King and Creator.

When we think about sin, there should be a pit in our stomachs and a deep gulp in our throats.

To be clear: sin isn't just something that happened to Adam and Eve, a long time ago in a distant world. We would have done the same thing in their place. This sin is now a part of all of us. Look at what Romans 5:12 says: "Therefore, just as sin entered the world through one man, and death through sin, and in this way death came to all people, because all sinned." The uncomfortable truth the Bible teaches is that we are all sinners (Rom. 3:23). We are sinners by nature and by choice. In other words, sin isn't only what we do. It's part of who we are.

We need to take sin seriously because of what it *is*. We also need to take sin seriously because of what it *does*, which brings us to our next point—the effects of sin.

Taking Sin Seriously: The Effects of Sin

Getting right to the point: Sin sends out a shockwave that has tainted everything about God's "very good" creation (Gen. 1:31). Nothing is left untouched.

The picture that's ingrained in me for this comes from a story when I was in the fourth or fifth grade. I was at a friend's house, and we were shooting BB guns at some empty, heavy duty metal coffee cans that we had set up against his garage. (By the way, shooting BBs at a metal target isn't a great idea. You'll see why in a second.) It's also important to mention they had just gotten a new sliding glass door at my friend's house. The targets were in front of us, and the sliding glass door was behind us, and off to the right. (You know what's going to happen.)

My friend—thankfully it was his house, and he was the one shooting—shot the BB gun at the target, and then the BB ricochetted off the target and hit the new sliding glass door. We heard it before we saw it. We could hear the spiderweb crack expand and by the time we looked behind us and saw the damage, the whole panel of the sliding glass door was covered by this spiderweb crack. My other friend and I just took off running. We left my friend who's house we were at to fend for himself. Thankfully, his parents were abundantly gracious.

Here's the mental picture I want to come back to: The whole door had been fractured by the impact of the BB.

That's what sin is! Sin fractures everything around us.

Just think of the story we get of God's good creation *before* Genesis 3. Humanity is in close communion with God. We see direct, personal interaction between humanity and God in the commands God gives—commands for humanity's flourishing (see Gen. 1:28–30; 2:16–17). God cares for Adam in providing a "helper suitable for him" (Gen. 2:18). Genesis 3:8 gives us the picture of God "walking in the garden in the cool of the day" with Adam and Eve—an intimacy and closeness we marvel at and long for when we read it. Again and again, a satisfying, enriching, whole, very good relationship between humanity and God stands out.

Humanity is in "very good" relationship with each other: It is "not good" for Adam to be alone and so God creates Eve. Human community is part of God's good design for His good creation. The "very good" human community we read about in Genesis 1–2 includes a beautiful complementarity, partnership, unity, and appreciation.

Humanity is also in a "very good" relationship with the surrounding creation. Humanity is given the command to "fill the earth and subdue it" (Gen. 1:28). This command finds additional color in Genesis 2:15, where God puts Adam in the garden of Eden and tells him to "work it and take care of it." The idea is one of tending—God's good garden should *stay good* because of humanity's care.[76] Commentators often mention how Adam and Eve would have eventually needed to *expand* the garden as they "filled the earth"—extending the reaches of this beautiful garden further and further out.[77] In all this, humanity's relationship with creation is characterized by a tending, caring stewardship, by purpose in work, and vision for expanding the garden.

Humanity is in "very good" relationship with God, with each other, with creation, and also with self. Genesis 2:25 underscores this clearly—highlighting that Adam and Eve felt "no shame." When we add everything we've seen already—confidence before God, close community with another, and clear purpose—all of these things contribute further to a whole and healthy view of self.

From top to bottom and at every angle, the picture we get from Genesis 1–2 is that creation is "very good."

And then the BB hits. Sin enters the world in Genesis 3. This "very good" creation is fractured. We've considered the "before" picture; now let's consider the "after" picture.

Humanity's relationship with God? Separation. Instead of running to God when He was walking in the Garden, Adam and Eve now hide from Him (Gen. 3:8). We find doubt instead of trust. Suspicion instead of security (Gen. 3:1–5). Instead of confidence before God there is now fear and shame (Gen. 3:10).

Humanity's relationship to each other? Blame and suspicion. Disordered relationships and bent desires. (See Gen. 3:12, 16–17.)

Humanity's relationship to creation? Brokenness and struggle. Pain in childbearing, as humanity fulfills the mandate to "fill the earth" (Gen. 3:16). Painful toil in working the ground, as humanity fulfills the mandate to "subdue the earth" (Gen. 3:17).

Our relationship to ourselves? Distorted and warped. Genesis 3 records the ripple effects of deserved guilt and shame that lead to fear, selfishness, self-deceit, and death—physical and spiritual.

The "after" picture I've presented here is bleak—and this only factors in what we learn from Genesis 3! As we continue the storyline of God's Word, the picture stays fractured as we see the effects of sin cascade deeply into every area we've been looking at: our relationship with God, with others, with creation, and within ourselves.

Why should we take sin seriously? Because of what it does—how it corrupts and fractures and warps everything it touches.

But we can't stop there. The Bible doesn't only diagnose our problem, it provides the solution. This brings us right into our final point.

Responding to Sin

The reality of sin demands a response. Do we succumb to it, shrugging our shoulders with indifference or hanging our head in defeat? Do we ignore it, hoping the problem will go away on its own? Do we hide it, pretending like the issue isn't really there? Do we embrace it and follow the spiral down as far as it can go? Of course the answer to these questions is a resolute "no."

Indeed, we see some of what *not* to do in Genesis 3—in Adam and Eve's response to sin. I've already mentioned a few of these already: They hide from God. They blame others. There's a turn inward—protecting self even if it means ignoring reality and distancing ourselves from our design.

These are all wrong ways to respond to sin—and we continue to see these wrong ways (and others) to respond to sin today. We see these wrong ways to respond to sin around us. And we see these wrong ways to respond to sin in us.

So what does a *right response* to sin look like?

Before we consider how we should respond to sin, let's reflect first on how God responds to sin in Genesis 3. To be sure, there were consequences. Adam and Eve both felt these consequences in their own way. Painful childbearing. Warped relationships. Toilsome labor. They're expelled from the garden. Even creation still feels these consequences of sin (Rom. 8:20–21). We can't get away from the reality that our sin does invite consequences.

But there's also grace. We see grace in Genesis 3:8–9— immediately following the record of Adam and Eve's sin in verses 6–7:

> Then the man and his wife heard the sound of the LORD God as he was walking in the garden in the cool of the day, and they hid from the LORD God among the trees of the garden. But the LORD God called to the man, "Where are you?" (Gen. 3:8–9)

God isn't "angry stomping" through the garden here, thrashing about while He's frustratedly searching for Adam. God's tone isn't one of unbridled rage. That mental picture would go against how God introduces Himself so clearly in Exodus 34:6–7a, that He is a "compassionate and gracious God, slow to anger, abounding in love and faithfulness, maintaining love to thousands, and forgiving wickedness, rebellion, and sin."

God doesn't ask this question in Genesis 3:9 because He doesn't know where Adam is. God knows where they are, and He knows what they did.

God isn't asking this question for Himself. He's asking it for Adam. He's drawing him out. Or better: Inviting him into continued relationship.

Sure, Adam responds the wrong way here in Genesis 3. But this doesn't change the grace God shows in inviting us out—into the light—to reengage in relationship with Him. When our sin is exposed and God draws us out in our sin—this "drawing out" isn't punishment; it's for restoration! This "drawing out" is grace!

I'll mention one more display of grace in Genesis 3, something God says in his pronouncement of curse on the serpent.

> And I will put enmity between you and the woman,
> and between your offspring and hers; he will crush
> your head, and you will strike his heel. (Gen. 3:15)

The serpent will strike the offspring of the woman (this indicates ongoing conflict between good and evil), but a future seed of the woman will crush the serpent. For thousands of years, since the earliest days of church history, theologians have called Genesis 3:15 the *protoevangelium*, or the "first gospel." It's here we see an early glimpse, from the lips of God Himself, that Satan doesn't win. He's defeated by the seed of the woman, who the New Testament ultimately reveals as Jesus Christ.[78]

Satan and sin don't win! Jesus wins. Grace wins.

Here's why I bring this up: The more we can see that God is still there in Genesis 3—He doesn't leave us in our sin but comes after us, with the goal of restoration—the more it invites our own right response to sin.

So now what do we do with all this? How should we respond to sin? Here are two takeaways.

One takeaway is that we **take sin seriously**—starting with the simple fact of owning our sin. We don't excuse our sin. Or justify it. Or ignore it. Or celebrate it. We call sin "sin." We see it the way God sees it, not the way our wrong desires or enemy wants us to see it. We understand that sin is destructive, not delightful. Our sin has separated us from God, and we can't save ourselves by ourselves. Practically, this means we're sensitive to deserved conviction over sin; we don't try to bury it. We genuinely grieve over what we've done—instead of just being sorry we got caught (2 Cor. 7:10–11).

This also means we take decided, intentional action to deal with sin in our lives—we repent, or we turn from sin. A rich theological word for this is the *mortification* of sin—we are putting sin to death (e.g., Rom. 6:11–14; Col. 3:5). We know that sin is "crouching at the door" and its desire is to "dominate you" (Gen. 4:7 NET). We cannot take a passive stance toward it. In the famous words of seventeenth-century Puritan writer John Owen, "Be killing sin or sin will be killing you."[79]

A second takeaway is that we **run to God** and pursue the things that honor Him—this is sometimes called *vivification* by theologians, where we are experientially growing into the new life available in Christ. Responding to sin isn't only *putting off* our old, sinful self and dealing with things that are clearly sinful; it's also *putting on* the new self that has been redeemed and renewed by Christ (Rom. 6:11–14, 17–18; Col. 3:9–10; see also 2 Cor. 5:17; Gal. 2:20). It's chasing the things of God and "being made new in the attitude of your minds," "put[ting] on the new self, created to be like God in true righteousness and holiness" (Eph. 4:23–24).

If you're reading this right now, that means God isn't done with you yet—He hasn't abandoned you! God is drawing you out. Where are you?

Some of you have never placed your faith in Jesus, but Genesis 3 has given you language to understand why you need God, and your heart is drawn to Him. You can start following Jesus today by understanding the gravity of your sin and turning from it (i.e., repentance), placing your faith in Jesus' finished work on the cross, and following Him as your Savior and Lord.

Some of you have been following Jesus for a long time but you've been ignoring sin in your life, and you know it's created a relational barrier between you and God—keeping you from experiencing the full life with Jesus that He's designed you for (see John 10:10). Acknowledge the gravity of your sin, confess it, and run to Jesus! Where are you?

As we respond to sin the right way, we don't have to wonder how God responds to us. The Bible tells us! We know how God responds (and it should fill us with gratitude and hope):

> If we confess our sins he is faithful and just and will forgive us our sins and purify us from all unrighteousness. (1 John 1:9)

This is such good news! When we respond to sin this right way, we know He receives us, and relationship is restored.

God's grace is greater than our sin.

ACKNOWLEDGMENTS

I've heard it said that "everyone has a book in them"—advancing the idea that people have stories to tell, wisdom to share, and perspective that can benefit others. Assuming for a minute that the saying has merit—that is, that everyone *does* have a book in them—I would also quickly add that it often takes others to pull that book out of them. Or that "the book inside of us" isn't yet in its final form but needs to itself be shaped by the relationships and networks around us.

In other words, yes—perhaps everyone does have a book in them. But for that book to see the light of day or the ink of print (or the glow of an e-reader), every author needs others.

If the importance of others is necessary for the *book* (singular) that everyone supposedly has inside of them, the value of others increases exponentially when authors go from one book to multiple *books* (plural). I have found that to be the case as I now complete my second book. With all this in mind, then, here is a small sampling of those I wish to thank—a sampling that represents the many who helped this writing project cross the finish line. (So many others could be listed!)

Thank you to Brookside Church, for the continuing encouragement to write—from church leadership, others on the staff team, and members of the congregation. Brookside, my books are written first with you in mind. It continues to be a privilege and an honor to serve alongside a godly team, with the congregation there, for the glory of God in the church and in Christ Jesus (Eph. 3:20–21).

Thanks to the numerous groups that have sat through classes and group settings where pieces of this book's material were developed and taught in seed form. These groups include pastor training in Zambia at the Hope Center, Brookside's 4D Church Leadership Program (4D!), and classes in the Brookside Institute.

Thank you to those ministry friends and churches that read my first book and have encouraged me to keep writing toward a second. Your conversations, texts, posts, and emails were fuel to my progress.

Thank you to the many who had a hand in moving this book through its various drafts. My editor, Connor Sterchi, helped make this book better through his careful eye and valuable suggestions. Connor, all throughout the process I felt like you were "for" this project and "for" me as a writer. Thank you. Thanks to Dr. Greg Carlson and Dr. Colby Kinser for reading early drafts of this book and providing helpful feedback. Thank you to Greg Carlson, Christina Dart, Colby Kinser, Matt LaPine, Jonathan Musonda, Emily Taylor, and Chris Winegar for your gracious endorsements. Any mistakes, ambiguities, or unintended omissions are my own.

Thanks to my family. Dad and Mom: As dad's physical health struggled during the writing of this book, know that I've seen how the vibrancy of your spiritual lives continues to shine in a life of prayer, strong dependence on God's Word, a deep care for others, and resilient faith in our Lord and Savior. Your examples remain a model to me of the fruit of faithfully practicing the spiritual disciplines. This book is dedicated to you.

And of course a huge thanks to Carrie and our four boys, Carston, Jadon, Sawyer, and Keller. You know I enjoy writing, and thanks for the ways you bear extra load to encourage that. But know that I always look forward most to our times together individually and together. Our Lord gifted me with each of you.

I end with gratitude to my Lord and Savior Jesus Christ. Apart from you I can do nothing. Thank you for your grace.

ABOUT THE AUTHOR

Tim Wiebe (MDiv, Trinity Evangelical Divinity School; DMin, Southern Baptist Theological Seminary) serves as the Pastor of Spiritual Formation at Brookside Church (EFCA) in Omaha, Nebraska. He and his wife, Carrie, have four sons.

NOTES

[1] ESPN, "The 150 greatest coaches in college football's 150-year history," December 10, 2019, https://www.espn.com/college-football/story/_/page/CFB150coaches/the-150-greatest-coaches-college-football-150-year-history.

[2] Tom Osborne, with Chad Bonham, *The Legacy of Leadership: Leading with the End in Mind* (Cross Training Publishing, 2023), 25.

[3] See Gerhard Kittel and Gerhard Friedrich, "ευσεβης" in *Theological Dictionary of the New Testament*, translated by Geoffrey W. Bromily, Vol VII, 175-85 (Eerdmans, 1971), 182-83.

[4] Tim Wiebe, *What Does It Mean to Follow Jesus?: A Clear, Biblical Picture of Discipleship* (self-published, 2024).

[5] Augustine, *Confessions*, trans. R. S. Pine-Coffin, Penguin Classics (Penguin, 1961), 21.

[6] Four worthwhile books that focus on the spiritual disciplines (listed here in no particular order) include Donald S. Whitney, *Spiritual Disciplines for the Christian Life*, rev. and updated (NavPress, 2014); Dallas Willard, *Spirit of the Disciplines: Understanding How God Changes Lives* (HarperOne, 1988), David Mathis, *Habits of Grace: Enjoying Jesus Through the Spiritual Disciplines* (Crossway, 2016); Matthew C. Bingham, *A Heart Aflame for God: A Reformed Approach to Spiritual Formation* (Crossway, 2025).

[7] See, e.g., Craig L. Blomberg, *Can We Still Believe the Bible? An Evangelical Engagement with Contemporary Questions* (Brazos, 2014); Greg Gilbert, *Why Trust the Bible?* (Crossway, 2015); Jonathan

Morrow, *Questioning the Bible: 11 Major Challenges to the Bible's Authority* (Moody, 2014); John Feinberg, *Light in a Dark Place: The Doctrine of Scripture*, Foundations of Evangelical Theology (Crossway, 2018).

⁸ See Ps. 119:16, 24, 35, 47, 70, 77, 92, 143, 174 (NIV). And that's just the simplest lexical observation. If we were to look at other ways the psalmist conveys delight in God's Word without using the word *delight* (e.g., vv. 48, 72, etc.), the number of references would increase substantially. See also next endnote.

⁹ e.g., Ps. 119:18, 97, 103, 111, 127, etc.

¹⁰ Grateful tip of the cap here to Derek Kidner, *Psalms 73–150*, TOTC (IVP Academic, 2009), 456–57. His content inspired this section.

¹¹ *Oxford English Dictionary*, s.v. "diligence (*n.*)," accessed July 2, 2024, https://www.oed.com/dictionary/diligence_n1?tab=factsheet#6801233.

¹² Thesaurus.com, s.v., "diligence," accessed July 2, 2024, https://www.thesaurus.com/browse/diligence.

¹³ For those that want to dig in more deeply than what I've included in the main body of the book, interested readers are directed to Andrew Abernathy, *Savoring Scripture: A Six-Step Guide to Studying the Bible* (IVP Academic, 2022); see also J. Scott Duvall and J. Daniel Hays, *Journey into God's Word: Your Guide to Reading ad Applying the Bible*, 2nd ed (Zondervan Academic, 2020); Craig G. Bartholomew and Michael W. Goheen, *The Drama of Scripture: Finding Our Place in the Biblical Story*, 3rd ed (Baker Academic, 2024).

¹⁴ Dallas Willard, *The Great Omission: Reclaiming Jesus's Essential Teachings on Discipleship* (HarperOne, 2006), 155.

¹⁵ A commentary is a book written to help you better understand books of the Bible. A good commentary will be written by someone who has studied that book at length. Commentaries will include helpful introductory comments on the book (e.g., identifying overarching themes and making comments about the cultural and literary context of the book) and work through individual verses or groups of verses to help draw out the author's original meaning. Good introductory commentary series include free access to The Gospel Coalition commentaries at https://www.thegospelcoalition.org/commentary/; the *God's Word for You* commentaries published by The Good Book Company; Tyndale Old Testament Commentaries and Tyndale New Testament Commentaries; and Pillar New Testament Commentaries. For those that want to explore commentary options more deeply, visit www.bestcommentaries.com.

---

¹⁶ Navigators, "The Word Hand Illustration," accessed April 9, 2025, https://www.navigators.org/resource/the-word-hand/.

¹⁷ Justin Taylor, "Do You Bleed Bibline?," The Gospel Coalition, August 11, 2011, https://www.thegospelcoalition.org/blogs/justin-taylor/do-you-bleed-bibline/.

¹⁸ J. I. Packer, *Knowing God* (InterVarsity, 1973), 32; italics added.

¹⁹ J. I. Packer and Carolyn Nystrom, *Praying: Finding Our Way through Duty to Delight* (IVP, 2006), 175.

²⁰ Used with Lorinda's permission, granted April 9, 2025, in personal correspondence.

²¹ Paul E. Miller, *A Praying Life: Connecting with God in a Distracting World* (NavPress, 2009), 20.

²² For a great resource getting further into Paul's prayers, see especially D. A. Carson, *Praying with Paul: A Call to Spiritual Reformation*, 2nd ed. (Baker Academic, 2015).

²³ Whitney, *Spiritual Disciplines for the Christian Life*, 191.

²⁴ Quoted in John Piper, *A Hunger for God: Desiring God through Fasting and Prayer* (Crossway, 1997), 16.

²⁵ John Mark Comer, *Practicing the Way: Be with Jesus. Become Like Him. Do as He Did.* (Waterbrook, 2024), 185.

²⁶ Quoted in Whitney, *Spiritual Disciplines*, 191.

²⁷ For anyone who may be newer to Old Testament studies, the Old Testament (or Hebrew Bible) was originally divided by the Hebrew people into three major divisions: the Law, the Prophets, and the Writings. See, e.g., Jason S. DeRouchie, ed, *What the Old Testament Authors Really Cared About: A Survey of Jesus' Bible* (Kregel Academic, 2013), 41–42.

²⁸ While the NIV says the Israelite community is to "deny themselves," and the ESV says they're to "afflict themselves," both translations include a footnote for this verse that renders the meaning of "fasting" plausible. See also G. J. Wenham, *The Book of Leviticus*, NICOT (Eerdmans, 1979), 305.

²⁹ Interested readers are encouraged to see Whitney, *Spiritual Disciplines*, 198–217 for his own thorough take on biblical purposes of fasting.

³⁰ Why do I focus here on fasting, and not sackcloth and ashes (which are also mentioned in this verse)? My best answer is simply because other biblical uses of fasting are not always accompanied by these other practices. These other practices perhaps seem to be more cultural and time-bound; fasting, on the other hand, carries across time in emphasis.

³¹ Whitney, *Spiritual Disciplines*, 207.

³² Tip o' the cap to Colby Kinser for mentioning this idea.

[33] Quoted in Whitney, *Spiritual Disciplines*, 2nd ed., 234–35.

[34] Quoted in Kevin DeYoung, *Crazy Busy: A (Mercifully) Short Book About a (Really) Big Problem* (Crossway, 2013), 83.

[35] Richard J. Foster, *Celebration of Discipline: The Path to Spiritual Growth* (HarperCollins, 1988), 97.

[36] Comer, *Practicing the Way*, 57.

[37] Foster, *Celebration of Discipline*, 97.

[38] Gareth Lee Cockerill, *The Epistle to the Hebrews*, NICNT (Eerdmans, 2012), 568.

[39] Cockerill, *Hebrews*, 569.

[40] See Walter A. Elwell and Robert W. Yarbrough, *Encountering the New Testament: A Historical and Theological Survey*, 2nd ed. (Baker Academic, 2005), 247.

[41] Quoted in Willard, *Spirit of the Disciplines*, 161.

[42] Wiebe, *What Does It Mean to Follow Jesus?* See esp. 129–30 for a brief summary of the six Cs. See also appendix 1 in the current volume.

[43] Careful readers will observe the possible rendering of "reflect" (instead of "contemplate") noted in some English versions. Most EVV seem to emphasize the contemplate side of this debate—so NIV, CSB, ESV, NKJV. See also Paul Barnett, *The Second Epistle to the Corinthians*, NICNT (Eerdmans, 1997), 205–9; also Ralph P. Martin, *2 Corinthians*, WBC 40 (Word Books, 1986), 71.

[44] "Band of Brothers (miniseries), Wikipedia, accessed March 12, 2024, https://en.wikipedia.org/wiki/Band_of_Brothers_(miniseries)#Awards_and_nominations.

[45] Alex Concepcion, ". . . but I served in a company of heroes." YouTube, May 27, 2103, 00:52, https://www.youtube.com/watch?v=tEjIIbOXqOk

[46] See Brad Harper and Paul Louis Metzger, *Exploring Ecclesiology: An Evangelical and Ecumenical Introduction* (Brazos, 2009), 41. My quote in the text is a paraphrase of Harper and Metzger here.

[47] For much more on this, readers are directed to my doctoral project, Tim Wiebe, "Establishing a Discipleship Pathway for Ministry Programming at Brookside Church, Omaha, Nebraska" (DMin project, The Southern Baptist Theological Seminary, 2022).

[48] See esp. D. A. Carson, "Worship Under the Word," in *Worship by the Book*, ed. D. A. Carson (Zondervan, 2002), 26. See pp. 26–58 for the fuller exposition of Carson's definition.

[49] See Wiebe, "Establishing a Discipleship Pathway," 47–49.

[50] For more on this, see esp. Colin Marshall and Tony Payne, *The Trellis and the Vine: The Ministry Mind-Shift That Changes Everything* (Matthias Media, 2024) or Colin Marshall and Tony Payne, *The Vine Project: Shaping Your Ministry Culture Around Disciple-Making* (Matthias Media, 2022). Also Wiebe, "Establishing a Discipleship Pathway" for more of my own work connecting the dots between these priorities and vibrant Christian growth. See also Comer, *Practicing the Way*, 160–62, though Comer uses the "trellis" image a bit more broadly related to a "rule of life." The imagery is certainly broad enough it can be used in various ways to support structure and systems to facilitate discipleship.

[51] See also Alex Mark, "Ready for Church: 5 Ways to Be Present in Worship," The Gospel Coalition, Feb 10, 2024, https://www.thegospelcoalition.org/article/ready-present-worship/.

[52] Collin Hansen and Jonathan Leeman, *Rediscover Church: Why the Body of Christ Is Essential* (Crossway, 2021), 145.

[53] See also Dallas Willard's memorable phrase, "Grace is opposed to earning, not to effort" in his *Great Omission*, 34.

[54] See 1 Thess 1:1-4; also 1 Cor 1:8-9. See also Gary S. Shogren, *1 & 2 Thessalonians*, ZECNT (Zondervan Academic, 2012), 233-34; Charles A. Wanamaker, *The Epistles to the Thessalonians*, NIGTC (Eerdmans, 1990), 207.

[55] Rankin Wilbourne, *Union with Christ: The Way to Know and Enjoy God* (David C. Cook, 2016), 43.

[56] Christopher W. Morgan and Thomas R. Schreiner, *Salvation*, Theology for the People of God (B&H Academic, 2024), 35; italics added.

[57] Wilbourne, *Union with Christ*, 55.

[58] Wilbourne, *Union with Christ*, 51.

[59] Edmund Clowney, "The Holy Spirit as Seal and Pledge," Ligonier, May 1, 1992, https://learn.ligonier.org/articles/the-holy-spirit-as-seal-and-pledge.

[60] See Eugene H. Peterson, *A Long Obedience in the Same Direction: Discipleship in an Instant Society* (InterVarsity, 2000), 11-22.

[61] Recommended, accessible English renditions of John Bunyan's *The Pilgrim's Progress* Alan Vermilye (Brown Chair Book, 2020), and C. J. Lovik (Crossway, 2019).

[62] Jim Collins, *How the Mighty Fall: And Why Companies Never Give In* (HarperCollins, 2009), 45–64. See also Dave Coffaro, "Organizational Strategy and Vision Drift," SmartBrief, March 17, 2020, https://www.smartbrief.com/original/organizational-strategy-and-vision-drift.

[63] Jeff Haden, "The 1 in 60 Rule: How Remarkably Successful People Stay on Track to Accomplish Their Biggest Goals," Inc., May 17, 2022, https://www.inc.com/jeff-haden/the-1-in-60-rule-how-remarkably-successful-people-stay-on-track-to-accomplish-their-biggest-goals.html.

[64] Rebecca Manley Pippert, *Stay Salt: The World Has Changed, Our Message Must Not* (The Good Book Company, 2020), 69.

[65] See for e.g. David G. Peterson, *The Acts of the Apostles*, PNTC (Eerdmans, 2009), 279. For another example of this organic spread of the gospel by everyday believers, see also Acts 11:19–21.

[66] Daryl Cripe, "Episode 634: Daryl Cripe on How to Reverse the Decline in Small, Mid-Size, and Stuck Churches, Reaching New People with No New Money, and How to Hit the Tipping Point in Church Revitalization," Interview by Carey Nieuwhof, https://careynieuwhof.com/episode634/.

[67] See more on this in Wiebe, *What Does It Mean to Follow Jesus?*, 116–19. Another great tool many use is the "3 Circles" Gospel Presentation and the accompanying "Life on Mission" app.

[68] Throughout the New Testament, the importance of community is reinforced through the dozens of "one another commands" addressed to the church. For much more on these one-another commands, see Tim Challies, "One Another—The Bible and Community," Challies.com, July 10, 2004, https://www.challies.com/articles/one-another-the-bible-community/.

[69] *The Fellowship of the Ring*, directed by Peter Jackson (New Line Cinema, 2001).

[70] Cornelius Plantinga Jr., *Not the Way It's Supposed to Be: A Breviary of Sin* (Eerdmans, 1996), ix.

[71] Plantinga, *Not the Way It's Supposed to Be*, ix, xiii.

[72] Plantinga, *Not the Way It's Supposed to Be*, xiii.

[73] See R. Kent Hughes, *Genesis*, Preaching the Word (Crossway, 2012), 67; also Allen P. Ross, *Creation and Blessing: A Guide to the Study and Exposition of Genesis* (Baker Academic, 1997), 134–35.

[74] See esp. Thaddeus Williams, "Oldest Lie in the Book: 'You Will Be Like God,'" The Gospel Coalition, Sept 7, 2022, https://www.thegospelcoalition.org/article/oldest-lie-be-like-god/.

[75] See Don Carson lecture, "Sin and the Fall," The Gospel Coalition, https://www.thegospelcoalition.org/sermon/sin-and-the-fall-genesis-3/.

[76] See, e.g., James Montgomery Boice, *Genesis: An Expositional Commentary Volume 1, Genesis 1:1-11:32* (Zondervan, 1982), 104. Also G. K. Beale, *The Temple and the Church's Mission: A Biblical Theology of the Dwelling Place of God*, NSBT (InterVarsity, 2004),

66–68; Timothy Keller, *Every Good Endeavor: Connecting Your Work to God's Work* (Dutton, 2012), 54–63.

[77] "The intention seems to be that Adam was to widen the boundaries of the Garden in ever-increasing circles by extending the order of the garden sanctuary into the inhospitable outer spaces. The outward expansion would include the goal of spreading the glorious presence of God" (Beale, *The Temple and the Church's Mission*, 85).

[78] See, e.g., R. Kent Hughes, *Genesis: Beginning the Blessing*, Preaching the Word (Crossway, 2004), 84–87; Derek Kidner, *Genesis*, TOTC (Inter-Varsity, 1967), 70–71.

[79] John Owen, *Overcoming Sin and Temptation*, ed. Kelly M. Kapic and Justin Taylor (Crossway, 2006), 50.

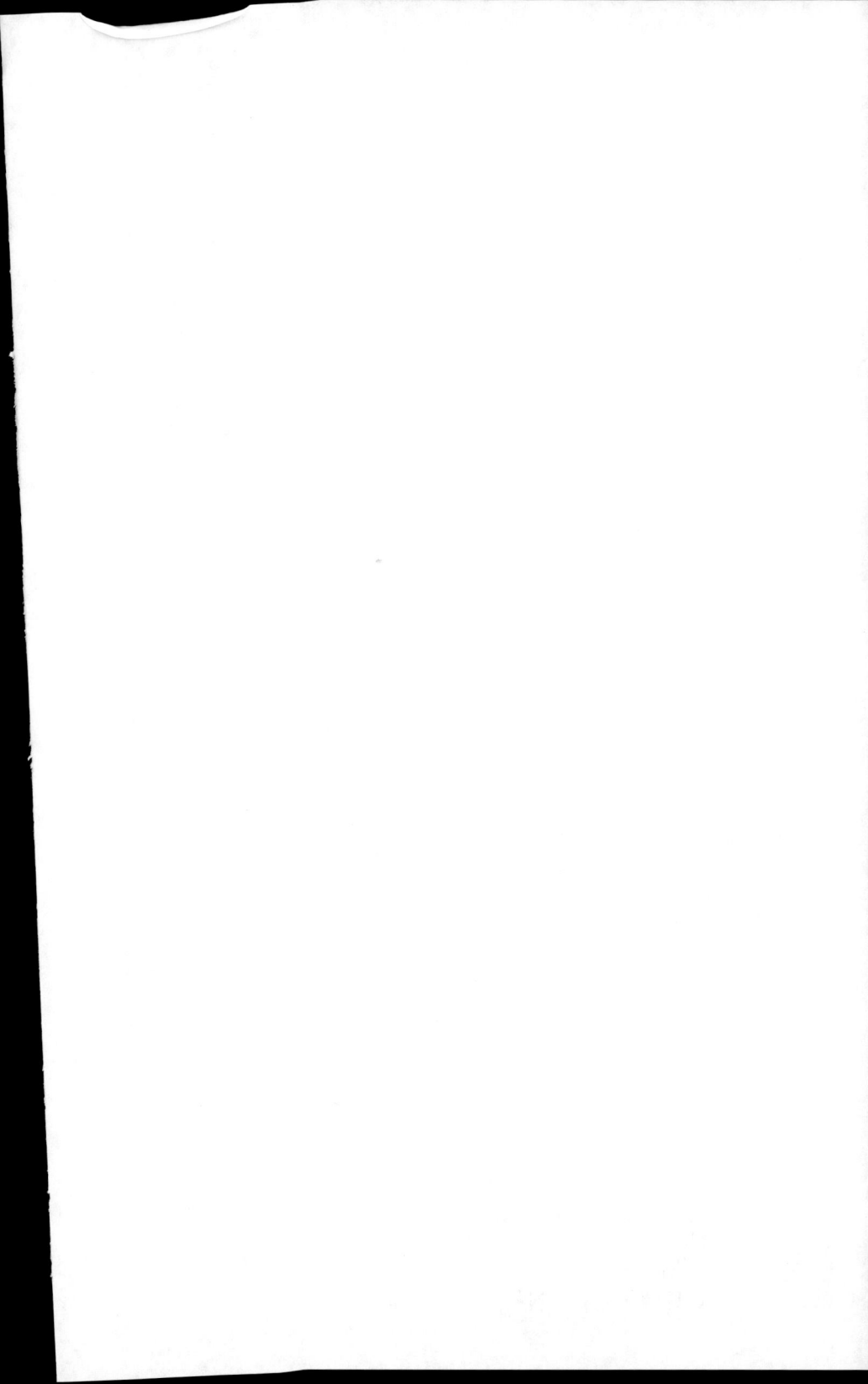

www.ingramcontent.com/pod-product-compliance
Lightning Source LLC
LaVergne TN
LVHW052024080426

835513LV00018B/2149